CROSSING THE YELLOW RIVER

The publication of this book was made possible, in part,
by the generous support of the
Witter Bynner Foundation for Poetry,
and the Dorothy and Henry Hwang Foundation.

CROSSING THE

Yellow River

THREE HUNDRED POEMS FROM THE CHINESE

Translated
with an Introduction by
Sam Hamill

Preface by
W. S. Merwin

BOA Editions, Ltd Rochester, NY 2000

First Edition
00 01 02 03   7 6 5 4 3 2 1

Publications by BOA Editions, Ltd.—a not-for-profit corporation under section
501 (c) (3) of the United States Internal Revenue Code—are made possible with
the assistance of grants from the Literature Program of the New York State
Council on the Arts, the Literature Program of the National Endowment for
the Arts, the Sonia Raiziss Giop Charitable Foundation, the Eric Mathieu King
Fund of The Academy of American Poets, The Halcyon Hill Foundation,
Starbucks Foundation, as well as from the Mary S. Mulligan Charitable Trust,
the County of Monroe, NY, and the Estate of E.M.K.

*   *   *

See page 280 for special individual acknowledgments.

Cover Design: Geri McCormick
Typesetting: Richard Foerster
Manufacturing: McNaughton & Gunn, Lithographers
BOA Logo: Mirko

Library of Congress Cataloging-in-Publication Data

Crossing the yellow river : 300 poems from the Chinese / translated and
introduced by Sam Hamill, with a preface by W.S. Merwin
    p. cm. -- (New American translation series ; vol. 13)
    ISBN 1–880238–97–7 -- 1–880238–98–5 (pbk.)
    1. Chinese poetry--Translations into English. I. Title: 300 poems from the
Chinese. II. Hamill, Sam. III. New American translation series ; vol. 13

PL2658.E3 C76 2000
895.1'1008--dc21

                                                                00-040338

BOA Editions, Ltd.
Steven Huff, Publisher
Richard Garth, Chair, Board of Directors
A. Poulin, Jr., President & Founder (1976–1996)
260 East Avenue
Rochester, NY 14604

www.boaeditions.org

To Eron Hamill
  who grew up with these poets;
to Gray Foster
  who brought light to Kage-an;

and to my coworkers at Copper Canyon Press:

In the heart of your heart, you know:
the mountains are high, the waters are wide.
  —Han Mu-shan

Contents

17   Preface by W. S. Merwin

22   Translator's Introduction: *Sustenance: A Life in Translation*

Early Poetry

37   Festal Song (Anonymous, *Shih Ching*)

38   War Lament (Anonymous, *Shih Ching*)

39   War Lament (Anonymous, *Shih Ching*)

40   Song (Li Yen-nien)

41   Lament (Cho Wen-chun)

42   Drinking Song (Ts'ao Ts'ao)

44   Song of Mount T'ai (Lu Chi)

45   The Lotus Lover (Tzu Yeh)

45   All Night (Tzu Yeh)

45   An End to Spring (Tzu Yeh)

46   A Smile (Tzu Yeh)

46   Illusions (Tzu Yeh)

47   An End to Spring (Tzu Yeh)

47   Late Spring (Tzu Yeh)

48   Bitter Harvest (Tzu Yeh)

48   Song (Tzu Yeh)

48   Song (Tzu Yeh)

49   Admonition (Tzu Yeh)

49   Busy in the Spring (Tzu Yeh)

50   Returning to My Fields and Gardens (T'ao Ch'ien)

51   Reply to Prefect Liu (T'ao Ch'ien)

52   To My Cousin, Ching-yuan, Twelfth Month, 403 (T'ao Ch'ien)

53   Passing Through Ch'ien-hsi, Third Month, 405 (T'ao Ch'ien)

54   Fire, Sixth Month, 408 (T'ao Ch'ien)

55   Lament (T'ao Ch'ien)

56   Drinking Alone in the Rainy Season (T'ao Ch'ien)

57   Crossing the Mountain, I Follow the Chin-chu River (Hsieh Ling-yun)

58   Visiting Pai-an Pavilion (Hsieh Ling-yun)
59   Climbing Stone Drum Mountain (Hsieh Ling-yun)
60   Written on the Lake While Returning to Stone Cliff
      Hermitage (Hsieh Ling-yun)
61   Complaint near the Jade Stairs (Hsieh T'iao)
62   Watching a Lonely Wild Goose at Nightfall (Hsiao Kang)
63   Bidding Farewell to Secretary Chou (Yu Hsin)
64   Farewell Poem (Anonymous)
65   Drinking Alone (Wang Fan-chih)
66   Poem (Wang Fan-chih)
67   In the Mountains (Wang Po)
68   View from Heron Tower (Wang Chih-huan)
69   Returning Late to Lu-men Shan (Meng Hao-jan)
69   Spring Dreams (Meng Hao-jan)
70   Silent at Her Window (Wang Ch'ang-ling)

Poems of Li Po

73   The Great Bird
73   In Memory of Ho Chi-chen
74   On Dragon Hill
74   Parting
75   Saying Good-bye in a Ch'in-ling Wineshop
75   Summer Days in the Mountains
76   Listening to a Flute on a Spring Night in Lo-yang
76   Longing for Someone
77   Drinking Wine with a Mountain Hermit
77   Taking Leave of a Friend
78   Ancient Airs
78   Farewell to Yin Shu
79   Remembering East Mountain
79   Fall River Song
80   Fall River Song
80   At Ch'ang-men Palace
81   Questions Answered
81   Mountain Drinking Song

82 Saying Good-bye to Meng Hao-jan at Yellow Crane Pavilion
82 To a Friend
83 In a Village by the River
83 Drinking Alone with the Moon
84 Return of the Banished
84 About Tu Fu
85 Going to Visit a Taoist Recluse on Heaven's Mountain Only to Find Him Gone
85 To the Tune: Beautiful Barbarian
86 Seeing Off a Friend
86 O-mei Mountain Moon
87 Crows at Dusk
87 Waterfall at Lu-shan
88 Old-Style Poem
88 Rising Drunk on a Spring Day
89 Complaint near the Jade Steps
89 Quiet Night Thoughts
90 Listening to a Flute in Yellow Crane Pavilion
90 Looking for Master Yung Ts'un near His Hermitage
91 Old Dust
91 Women of Yueh
92 Blue Water
93 To Tu Fu from Shantung
93 Springtime South of the Yangtze
94 Remembering Ancient Days in Yueh
94 Zazen on Ching-t'ing Mountain

Poems of Wang Wei
97 Birdsong Valley
97 Visiting the Mountain Hermitage of a Monk at Gan-hua Monastery
97 Sitting Alone on an Autumn Night
98 Mourning for Yin Yao
99 At Li's Mountain Hermitage

99   Chi River Gardens and Fields
100   Deer Park
100   At Lake Yi
100   The Way to the Temple
101   Crossing the Yellow River
101   Sailing Down the Han
102   Reply to a Magistrate
102   At a House in the Bamboo Grove
103   Return to Wang River
103   At the Hermitage of Master Fu
104   Hermitage at Chung-nan Mountain
104   A Meal for the Monks

Poems of Tu Fu

109   Sunset
109   Random Pleasures (I)
110   Random Pleasures (II)
110   Rising Spring Waters
111   Evening near Serpent River
111   Descending Through Dragon Gate
112   Dragon Gate Gorge
113   Yen-chou City Wall Tower
113   New Year's Eve at the Home of Tu Wei
114   Looking at Mount T'ai
114   Leaving Ch'in-chou
115   Passing Mr. Sung's Old House
115   Visiting the Monastery at Lung-men
116   Going to the Palace with a Friend at Dawn
116   Taking Leave of Two Officials
117   To Li Po on a Spring Day
117   River Pavilion
118   Random Pleasures (III)
118   Random Pleasures (IV)
119   After Rain
119   The Draft Board at Shih-hao

121 Song of the War Wagons
122 To Li Po on a Winter Day
122 Moon on the Cold Food Festival
123 Moonlit Night
123 Lament for Ch'en T'ao
124 Word from My Brothers
124 Passing the Night
125 Poem for Mr. Li in Early Spring
125 Farewell Rhyme
126 P'eng-ya Road
128 The Journey North
134 Sent to the Magistrate of P'eng-chou
134 Leaving Government Offices
134 Another Spring
135 Drinking at Crooked River
136 Crooked River Meditation
136 Drinking with Elder Cheng the Eighth at Crooked River
137 To Abbot Min the Compassionate
137 Dreaming of Li Po
139 Heavenly River
139 Thinking of Li Po
140 Watching the Distances
140 Ch'iang Village
141 The Cricket
141 Listless
142 Firefly
142 Sick Horse
143 Empty Purse
143 Departing from Ch'in-chou
144 Impromptu
145 Song of T'ung-ku
145 Becoming a Farmer
146 The Servant Boy Delivers
146 In a Village by the River
147 Early Rising
147 To a Guest

148   Homestead
148   In Seclusion
149   The Madman
149   A Hundred Worries
150   Random Pleasures (V)
150   Random Pleasures (VI)
151   Random Pleasures (VII) ·
151   Random Pleasures (VIII)
151   Random Pleasures (IX)
152   Evening after Rain
152   Song for a Young General
152   After Solstice
153   In Praise of Rain
154   Singing Girls (Written in Jest)
155   Clear after Rain
155   Poem for My Brother Returning to My Farm
156   Spring Homecoming
157   Lone Wild Goose
157   I Stand Alone
158   The Thatched Hut
161   After the Harvest
161   Moon, Rain, Riverbank
162   Running from Trouble
162   A Broken Boat
163   Facing the Snow
164   Traveler's Pavilion
164   On a Portrait of a Falcon
165   Homage to the Painter General Ts'ao
165   Sleepless Nights
166   Night in a Room by the River
166   Night Thoughts While Traveling
167   A Summit
167   To My Younger Brother
168   By Yangtze and Han
168   At the Thatched Hall of the Ts'ui Family
169   Facing the Snow

169   Six Choruses
171   Heading South

Poems of Po Chu-i, Yuan Chen, and Others
175   Listening to a Flute at Night near the City Wall (Li Yi)
176   Despair (Meng Chiao)
177   Elegy (Chang Chi)
178   Blacktail Row (Liu Yu-hsi)
179   After Reading Lao Tzu (Po Chu-i)
179   To Yuan Chen (Po Chu-i)
179   On a Portrait of the Poet (Po Chu-i)
180   Night Duty in the Palace, Dreaming of a Hsien-yu
       Temple (Po Chu-i)
181   To a Young Widow (Po Chu-i)
181   Reading Yuan Chen on a Boat (Po Chu-i)
182   Cold Night (Po Chu-i)
182   River Flute (Po Chu-i)
183   In the Shadows of the Wu-t'ung Tree (Anonymous)
184   Snowy River (Liu Tsung-yuan)
185   White Dress (Yuan Chen)
185   Oriole (Yuan Chen)
186   Peach Blossoms (Yuan Chen)
186   Letter Smuggled in a Fish (Yuan Chen)
186   When We Are Apart (Yuan Chen)
187   Three Dreams in Chiang-ling (Yuan Chen)
190   Dreaming of My Wife (Yuan Chen)
190   Retirement (Yuan Chen)
191   Remembering (Yuan Chen)
191   Bamboo Mat (Yuan Chen)
191   Elegy (Yuan Chen)
193   Empty House (Yuan Chen)
194   Elegy (Anonymous)
195   Requiem (Wang Fan-chih)
195   Reclusive (Wang Fan-chih)
196   Lament for a Courtesan (Li Ho)

196 Song: Green Water, Singing Girl (Li Ho)
197 Drinking All Night, Sleeping All Day (Li Ho)
198 Days of Rain (Li Ho)
198 The Lute Player (Li Ho)
199 Life at the Capital (Li Ho)
199 Melancholic (Li Ho)
200 A Country Road (Li Ho)
201 Departing in Early Morning (Tu Mu)
202 Alone Beside the Autumn River (Li Shang-yin)
202 From the Heights (Li Shang-yin)

The Rise of Tzu Poetry

205 To the Tune: Southern Song (Wen T'ing-yun)
205 To the Tune: The Water Clock (Wen T'ing-yun)
206 To the Tune: Beautiful Barbarian (Wei Chuang)
207 Against Conscription (Wei Chuang)
208 To the Tune: The Wine Spring (Li Hsun)
209 To the Tune: The Wine Spring (Li Hsun)
210 To the Tune: In the Hills (Hsueh Chao-yun)
211 Oriole Song (Hsueh Chao-yun)
212 Lu-lung Village, Autumn (Hsu Hsuan)
213 To the Tune: Beautiful Lady Yu (Li Yu)
214 To an Ancient Tune (Anonymous)
215 Springtime South of the Yangtze (K'o Chun)
216 Song (Liu Yung)
216 Song (Liu Yung)
217 Song (Liu Yung)
217 Song (Liu Yung)
218 Lament (Liu Yung)
220 Cicada Song (Liu Yung)
222 Song (Yen Shu)
223 The Lice (Mei Yao-ch'en)
224 Necessities (Mei Yao-ch'en)
225 A Cutting (Ou-yang Hsiu)
226 Working for the Government (Wang An-shih)

226 Night Watch (Wang An-shih)
227 On Chung Mountain (Wang An-shih)
227 At Home (Wang An-shih)
227 Spring Evening on Pan Mountain (Wang An-shih)
228 Hui-chu Temple, Mount K'un (Wang An-shih)
229 Climbing Yun-lung Mountain (Su Tung-p'o)
229 At the Temple of Kuan Yin in the Rain (Su Tung-p'o)
230 Rain During the Cold Food Festival (Su Tung-p'o)
230 Remembering My Wife (Su Tung-p'o)
232 Sleepless (Ch'in Kuan)
232 From a Dream (Ch'in Kuan)
233 Song (Ch'in Kuan)
233 Farewell Song (Ch'in Kuan)
235 Peach Blossom Stream (Chou Pang-yen)
236 To an Ancient Tune (Chu Tun-ju)
237 To the Tune: Happiness Approaches (Li Ch'ing-chao)
237 To the Tune: Sands of the Washing Stream (Li Ch'ing-chao)
238 To the Tune: Partridge Sky (Li Ch'ing-chao)
238 An End to Spring (Li Ch'ing-chao)
239 To the Tune: Partridge Sky (Li Ch'ing-chao)
239 To the Tune: Bodhisattva's Headdress (Li Ch'ing-chao)
240 To the Tune: Magnolia Blossoms (Li Ch'ing-chao)
240 To the Tune: Lips Painted Red (Li Ch'ing-chao)
241 To the Tune: Drunk in Flower Shadows (Li Ch'ing-chao)
242 To the Tune: Eternal Joy (Li Ch'ing-chao)
243 To the Tune: Happiness Approaches (Li Ch'ing-chao)
243 To the Tune: Plum Blossoms (Li Ch'ing-chao)
244 To the Tune: Spring at Wu Ling (Li Ch'ing-chao)
245 To the Tune: Butterflies Love Flowers (Li Ch'ing-chao)
246 To the Tune: Sands of the Washing Stream (Li Ch'ing-chao)
246 To the Tune: Boat of Stars (Li Ch'ing-chao)
247 To an Ancient Tune (Yao K'uan)
248 To the Tune: Beautiful Barbarian (Anonymous)

Later Poems

251   Mural, Ch'ien-ming Temple (Lu Yu)
252   Song (Anonymous)
253   Love Song (Hu Chih-yu)
254   Love Song (Ma Chih-yuan)
254   In Autumn (Ma Chih-yuan)
255   Evening Bells near a Temple (Ma Chih-yuan)
256   At Waterfall Temple (Chang K'o-chiu)
256   Year's End (Chang K'o-chiu)
257   T'ung Pass (Chang Yang-hao)
258   Taoist Song (Teng Yu-pin)
258   Taoist Song (Teng Yu-pin)
259   Taoist Song (Teng Yu-pin)
260   Love Song (Ch'iao Chi)
261   Autumn on the Riverbank (Chao Shan-ch'ing)
262   On Love (Hsu Tsai-ssu)
263   Love Song (Kuan Yun-shih)
264   A Traveler's Life (Sung Fang-hu)
265   Song of Parting (Wang Po-ch'eng)
266   Magic City Monastery (Wang Yang-ming)
266   Taoist Song (Wang Yang-ming)

267   Notes on the Poets
277   Acknowledgments
278   About the Translator
280   Colophon

Preface

Along with all the reminders that we have had, and should have, of the inevitable distance between the musical and cultural conventions of any originals and English refractions of them, the eighty years since Arthur Waley's *170 Chinese Poems* (published in 1918) have produced an imposing dynasty of translators of Chinese poetry. These translations, in turn, have had a subtle but pervasive influence on poetry written in English during that time.

Sam Hamill's work began some fifty years after Waley's volume, and Ezra Pound's Chinese translations, appeared. His Introduction gives an illuminating account of his relation to what had become, by mid-century, a tradition of translating Chinese poetry. We might recall, briefly, how that tradition, which provides the setting for Sam Hamill's translations, evolved.

In the years just before World War I, and then—hard as it is to imagine—during that war, both Helen Waddell and Arthur Waley were working on translations of ancient Chinese poetry. Fashions in literature are as insubstantial as other images of fortune, and there are probably few who now read Waddell's *Lyrics from the Chinese*, the Georgian poems she composed from prose translations she had found in Legge's *The Chinese Classics*, which had been based on Latin translations made by a French Jesuit, Père Lacharme, in the eighteenth century.

Legge's translations of Confucius were of importance to Pound, who spoke of them with respect. And it would be unjust to dismiss Waddell's poems, remote as they were from their thousand-year-old originals. The Georgian lyrics she made of them are frequently lovely and give a sense of the originals as songs. Their representation of the nature of eighth-century Chinese poetry is, indeed, vague, tinted in the mode of the pre-Raphaelites, with a touch of the exoticism of Edward Fitzgerald's *Rubaiyat*. They relay echoes of English lyrics from as far back as the Elizabethan songbooks and the border ballads, and exhibit—often with grace of language and feeling—conventions that were thoroughly familiar in English.

But they were probably no more remote from the conventions of the originals than Ben Jonson's *Drink to me only with thine eyes* was from its Latin source, or Alexander Pope's *Iliad* from Homer's hexameters.

Arthur Waley began with something else in mind. Whereas Helen Waddell's enviable erudition was focused on Latinate Europe, Waley was determined to learn Chinese and hear for himself what might be there. His arrival at that passion and his pursuit of it were to become important to the history of poetry in English. In great part, it seems, he taught himself. Though that cannot be the whole story, he must have been following some guiding note of his own all the way, for others whose native tongue was English learned Chinese in Waley's own generation, but no one else produced translations like his.

By the time Waley came to write his preface to *170 Chinese Poems* he was able to describe, in hindsight, the intentions that he had evolved. "I have aimed at literal translation, not paraphrase. . . . Considering imagery to be the soul of poetry, I have avoided either adding images of my own or suppressing those of the original. . . . Any literal translation of Chinese poetry is bound to be to some extent rhythmical, for the rhythm of the original obtrudes itself. . . . I have, therefore, tried to produce regular rhythmic effects similar to those of the original. . . . I have not used rhyme because it is impossible to produce in English rhyme effects at all similar to those of the original. . . ."

It is worth paying attention to those principles that Waley had formulated for himself. Although some of them have been questioned on one count or another, what he accomplished in that volume was revolutionary—a breakthrough not only for the translation of classical Chinese poetry into English, but for translation of poetry altogether, and for English poetry itself. From Pound to Eliot to the present day it is impossible to imagine poetry in English without the presence and example of Waley's Chinese poems.

Sam Hamill's work, like Waley's, represents a lifetime's devotion to the classic originals, which survived in a long, subtle, intricate current. Hamill draws, with erudition, gratitude, and years of fond listening, upon two traditions at once. The great Chinese poets, for all their formality and regard for conventions, speak often with a directness which make them seem surprisingly intimate and close to us. Some of this is clearly at the heart of a note of thankful affection. We sense Hamill's relation to these poets through how he weighs the poems syllable by syllable before trying to hear syllables for them in English.

I honor his meticulous concern to convey into English what the original is actually saying, and to do so while remaining aware of what the form accomplishes in Chinese. And at the same time Hamill's allegiance to his own ear, his willingness to wait and alter until the sound rings true, and the sense of the original is audible as a poem in English that in some crucial way represents the poem in Chinese.

One cannot do better than to look to Hamill's representations of Tu Fu for the true note.

In Praise of Rain

We suffered drought, months without rain.
Then, this morning, clouds climbed from the river:

misty rain began to drizzle,
falling in every direction.

Birds returned to their nests,
forest flowers freshened all their colors.

Now, at dusk, the rains continue their song
and I want to hear it all night long.

Song of T'ung-ku

Already old, and still without a name,
I've starved three years in these mountains.

The ministers of Ch'ang-an all are young,
their money and honors earned.

My friends, the mountain sages,
dwell only on the past, in their hurting.

I chant this last song sadly, my eyes
on the August sky where the white sun races.

The great treasure of classic Chinese poetry is not composed of its variety of subjects nor even of a wide range of feeling, but of the depth and clarity and delicacy with which subjects—often familiar ones—and feelings are evoked. In Hamill's own poetry, as well as in the body of translations that he has produced over thirty years, there is a directness of feeling, a trust in plainness and simplicity, that must be typical of the great exemplars of periods of Chinese poetry. Some of his poems address poets from the Chinese tradition: forebears, models and companions. Some of them, of course, present subjects far removed from the settings of the Chinese poets. Here's a favorite which seems to look both ways:

Seated Figure

It is a long way from there to here.
It is longer than all the old roads of exile,
longer even than the silence of the heron.
The landscapes changed. Someone
numbered the dead, someone mapped the pain.

Once, they say, the animals came to us,
and licked our palms for the salt,
and looked at us with huge, knowing eyes,
then turned and left
alone. And entered Paradise.

The true scholar's humility can be heard in Hamill's own poems as well as in his translations. His work is an example of the way poetry and translation have come to inform each other in our time. Since I am not an Asian linguist I must take his knowledge of the originals on faith, but the nature of his devotion to his sources leaves me in no doubt. All of us who cannot read classical Chinese are in Sam Hamill's debt for this assembly of translations which years of patience and listening have brought to life in English.

—W. S. Merwin

Translator's Introduction
Sustenance: A Life in Translation

I was introduced to classical Chinese poetry by Kenneth Rexroth and the Beat poets in the late 1950s, especially by Rexroth's immensely popular *One Hundred Poems from the Chinese*, which included thirty-odd poems translated from Tu Fu, whom Rexroth called "the greatest non-epic, non-dramatic poet in history." I drew inspiration from what I learned of Han Shan from Jack Kerouac's *The Dharma Bums* and Gary Snyder's translations, and from the poets in Robert Payne's *The White Pony*, Witter Bynner's translations, and of course those of Arthur Waley.

Later, after four years in the Marine Corps, two of which were spent in Japan where I began Zen practice and learned some rudimentary Japanese, I came to Ezra Pound's adaptations from the notebooks of Ernest Fenollosa, published as *Cathay* in 1915. In an essay in *A Poet's Work* (2nd Ed., Carnegie-Mellon University Press, 1998), "On the Making of Ezra Pound's Cathay," I discuss the origins and development of this little volume of only fourteen poems, claiming it as the single most influential volume of poetry in this century. I won't reiterate in depth here, but will elucidate a few of Pound's problems because they reveal some of the dangers of translating without knowledge of the original.

Fenollosa knew little Japanese and almost no Chinese. His informants were two Japanese professors, Mori and Ariga, neither of whom were fluent in classical Chinese, and thus Li Po became known in the west by his Japanese name, Rihaku. This trilingual effort sometimes produced strange results, as in "Separation on the River Kiang." Pound retains Fenollosa's Japanese pronunciation, *ko-jin*, meaning simply "person," mistakenly treating it as a personal name rather than recognizing the two Chinese characters as *ku jen* in the original meaning. The *kiang* in the title means "river." So Pound's title becomes "Separation on the River River" rather than "Separation on the Yangtze River" as in the original. Nevertheless, *Cathay* opened the doors to American modernism. More than any other volume, it is responsible for the personal tone of much of this century's shorter lyrical verse rooted in imagism.

When I began translating Tu Fu in the mid-1970s, I began by looking up each character and annotating each poem before attempting my own draft, then turning to translations by Florence Ayscough, William Hung, Rexroth, and others for comparative readings. What I found was often surprising.

Here is my translation of Tu Fu's "New Year's Eve at the Home of Tu Wei":

> Seeing the year end at a brother's home,
> we sing and toast with pepper wine.
>
> The stable is noisy with visitors' horses.
> Crows abandon trees lit by torches.
>
> Tomorrow morning I turn forty-one.
> The slanting sunset shadows lengthen.
>
> Why should one exercise self-restraint?
> I may as well stay drunk all the days of my life.

Rexroth, who is very good at locating the personal voice and situation of Tu Fu in his translations, makes no effort at recapturing the formal end-stopped couplets of the original. The couplet is the fundamental unit of classical Chinese poetry and Tu Fu its greatest master. Choosing in its stead a typically loose line that may be a run-on, Rexroth's version ends:

> In the winter dawn I will face
> My fortieth year. Borne headlong
> Towards the long shadows of sunset
> By the headstrong, stubborn moments,
> Life whirls past like drunken wildfire.

Sometimes Rexroth relies too heavily on Ayscough or on the French translations of Hervey de Saint-Denys or Georges Margoulies. In this instance he is clearly led astray by the former. Ayscough's translation reads:

At bright dawn my years will bridge four tens;
I fly, I gallop towards the slanting shadows of sunset.
Who can alter this, who can bridle, who restrain the moments?
Fiery intoxication is a life's career.

While Rexroth's version makes a fine poem in English, Ayscough's version carries considerable Victorian baggage. Neither poem, I believe, captures the spirit of Tu Fu very successfully. Tu Fu's poem is not about "fiery intoxication." It is not about life whirling past or the pathetic fallacy, "drunken wildfire." Hung's version:

To see the year depart at a brotherly home,
To participate in the songs and toasts with the pepper-wine,
I can hear from the stable the noisy horses of the guests,
I can see the crows leaving the trees because of the torches.

By tomorrow, I shall no longer be forty;
The evening of life will be fast coming upon me.
Of what use is it to be cautious and to exercise restraint?
Let me forget it all by being utterly drunk.

If Hung is wordy, he is closest to the original. If his penultimate line is far too prosy, the ultimate line is far too generalized. He also inserts an intrusive "I can hear" and "I can see" where there is none in the original. Sometimes a first or second person pronoun needs to be added in translation, but one should do so only when essential.

Hung also contributes elsewhere to general misunderstanding, as when he translates a line in what is probably Tu Fu's last suite of poems, "Such is indeed the shining grace of God." Tu Fu had no concept of a monotheistic god. The principle religions of China in the eighth century were Taoism and Buddhism, neither of which accommodates any notion of a monolithic god. Master Tu was a good Confucian in many respects, not a deeply religious man. Rather he demonstrated a decidedly existential turn of mind. Hung allowed western civilization to intrude upon eastern art in a notably ugly sentence.

Tu Fu's joy in joining his brother is shaded by deep resignation as the poet considers the conditions of his life. What is implied in the original, and what should be brought into English, is the notion that somehow, being Tu Fu, he will not waste away sitting before the wine jug. The great poet-out-of-office, unsung in his own time, asks the question every poet asks under such circumstances: Why do we do it? Why not give up and submit to self-despondency or the numbing effects of wine? The Chinese poet is not embarrassed by direct expression of his emotion or conflict.

Another way translators sometimes go wrong is by investing too much in the pictographic elements of characters. Although an excellent essay, the Pound-Fenollosa "Chinese Written Character as a Medium for Poetry" leads many a westerner to forget that the Chinese language, like others, is a spoken tongue, and that its poetry, like our own, aspires to the conditions of music. One of the things immediately lost in translation is the ability to bring the play of pictographic elements within words into English. But if we remember that Chinese poetry was chanted, then we can remember how important is the ear in poetry.

There is not much we can do with a basically monosyllabic, rhymed five-or-seven-character line in American English. Attempts to translate classical Chinese into rhymed English metrical structures have largely resulted in academic doggerel. In translating Chinese poetry, I sought formality enough to represent the couplet by couplet construction of the original, including the syntactical parallelism where possible, and to interpret or interpolate within the poem only where I deemed it essential. Chinese has an almost infinitely larger capacity for rhyming than English. I sought therefore to pay particular attention to assonance and consonance, slant and implied rhyme, while struggling to be true to what I perceived to be what the poet said and the spirit in which his poem is given, meaning the general tone and stance.

I learned early to rely on scholars whose knowledge of classical Chinese is far greater than mine. After nearly ten years on Tu Fu, I completed a first draft manuscript of about one hundred of his poems. A university press editor asked Irving Yucheng Lo to evaluate my work. Professor Lo was kind enough to comment on each poem, noting exactly where I had misread a Chinese character or misinterpreted a line. His generous offering of time and scholarship was encouragement enough for me to rework the manuscript.

Here is one of Tu Fu's last poems:

Transliteration:

Chun an tao hua shui
yun fan feng shu lin
tou sheng liang hi ti
shi yuan geng zhan jin
lao bing nan zheng ri
jan en bei wang xin
bai nian ge zi ku
wei jien you zhi yin

Heading South

Spring returns to Peach Blossom River
and my sail is a cloud through maple forests.

Exiled, I lived for years in secret, moving on
farther from home with tear-stains on my sleeves.

Now old and sick, at last I'm headed south.
Remembering old friends, I look back north a final time.

A hundred years I sang my bitter song,
but not a soul remembers those old rhymes.

I am perhaps guilty of explicating too much by adding the "living in secret" where the original suggests simply "refugee." In addition to wanting to do more than just call up the image of the refugee, I needed to fill out the line musically, and I think the interpolation is helpful. I think it is an important poem and have been surprised that other recent translators of Tu Fu have ignored it.

After years in exile, the old poet thought he was about to return home. He was still virtually unpublished and unknown but to a few poet-friends. The resignation and frustration articulated in this poem has been given a deeply ironic turn by the judgment of history. The poet died shortly thereafter, never dreaming that he might one day be declared the greatest poet in the history of Chinese.

While completing translation work on Tu Fu's *Facing the Snow*, I translated a small selection of the Tzu Yeh songs and poems by Li Ch'ing-chao, *The Lotus Lovers,* about fifty poems by Li Po, *Banished Immortal*, and Lu Chi's *Wen Fu: The Art of Writing*. I found the *Wen Fu* to be particularly helpful, not only as a translator's handbook, but as a writer's. "When studying the work of the masters, watch the working of their minds." Lu Chi was among the first poets to discuss form and content in poetry, and he lays out an elegant tradition, a good deal of which may be applied directly to our own practice two millennia and another language later. In each instance my translations were corrected, improved and clarified by being passed under the eyes of such knowledgeable scholar-translators as J. P. Seaton, with whom I translated *The Essential Chuang Tzu.*

I was fortunate to receive a Japan-U.S. Fellowship in 1988 and spent much of that year following Bashō's famous route through Japan's northern interior as I began to translate his *Oku no hosomichi, Road to the Interior,* now included in the more comprehensive *Narrow Road to the Interior, & Other Writings* (Shambhala). When I began going to school on Bashō, I had thought haiku was something I would study for perhaps a year. Ten years later, finally seeing my book into print, I realized that I would continue to be Bashō's student for the rest of my life. The work is never finished. Every translation is a provisional conclusion.

While I knew that my studies in Chinese would be helpful, just how helpful became clear almost immediately. Bashō's poems and prose are loaded with paraphrases and quotations and echoes drawn from Chuang Tzu and Tu Fu and Po Chu-i. All during his twenties and thirties, Bashō went to school on Tu Fu. He claimed to have carried a copy of *Chuang Tzu* with him wherever he went. To know the working of his mind, it is helpful to read what he read, to understand as much as possible about his Zen practice and the social conditions and traditions within which he came to flower.

Japanese poetry flows from two forms, the *choka* or longer poem, and *waka* or shorter poem. Over a millennia of aesthetic discussion and development, the *waka* evolved into *tanka*, both written in syllabic lines of 5-7-5-7-7 respectively. Unlike Chinese, Japanese is polysyllabic, and its sounds are much closer to western languages than the former. The Japanese language combines *kanji*, Chinese written characters, with a forty-odd character phonetic syllabary, *kana*. Tanka and haiku translated literally usually come out a few syllables shorter in English than in the original Japanese. Consequently, most western translators have simply ignored the syllabic structure, thereby sacrificing the musicality that may be achieved by adhering to form.

Another, and to my mind much more egregious, mistake on the part of many translators is to rearrange the order of perception in a poem, often with the intent of creating a kind of formal closure of the poem. From R. H. Blyth's renowned scholarship of the thirties to recent versions, one sees this unfortunately common practice. Haiku often opens at the end, rather than closing. Basho's most famous poem, for example:

> Furuike ya
> kawazu tobikomu
> mizu no oto

> At the ancient pond
> a frog plunges into
> the sound of water

How this poem has suffered in English! I can't remember whose version, nor can I locate it now, but years ago I read one that went:

> An old pond.
> A frog leaps in.
> Kerplop!

The "translator" wanted a punch line at the end. If we may assume that the translator knew what the original actually said, perhaps this ultimate line is an attempt to achieve onomatopoeia. The result may be economical, but completely misses the whole point Basho is making. This translation remains true to the order of perception, but ruins the poem by creating artificial closure. *Mizu* is water; *no* is prepositional; *oto* is sound. "The sound of water." Every translator who has put this frog (*kawazu*) into water has missed the poetry. The frog plunges, a word I chose because of its onomatopoeia in the context of leaping into water, into pure sound. I wanted to stay close to the original form, remaining true to Bashō's ultimate line, a line, I propose, that is followed by a fourth unwritten line of silence. The poem opens at the end, leaving the reader-listener listening.

Some say the haiku is indebted to the four-line Chinese *chueh-chu*, and that by leaving out the third line, an imaginative leap is made. I doubt the accuracy of such a theory, but there are some structural similarities. Bashō, like his Chinese predecessor, often sets a scene in the first line, but uses the Japanese "cutting word" *ya* to create a kind of emphasis, "At the ancient pond, yes, / a frog," etc. He then discovers a revelation. The *chueh-chu* also makes use of an imaginative leap, usually between the third and fourth lines. But there similarities end. The Chinese poet has no cutting word, but often makes use of surprising juxtaposition.

Another example:

> Fuyuniwa ya
> tsuki mo ito naru
> mushi no gin

A winter garden—
the moon also a thread,
like the insect's song

What does that *mo* ("also") in the second line refer to? If the moon (*tsuki*) is "also a thread," what is the first thread? The insect's (*mushi no gin*) song? Chuang Tzu often speaks of "running out the string of our days." Perhaps Bashō means the thread of his own life. The ambiguity is there in the original, and to fail to represent that complexity is to fail in the service of poetry. One implication might be that the moon is the thread stitching the winter garden to the insect's song. Where there is a deliberate use of ambiguity in the original, I have tried to create a parallel in translation.

Sometimes the translator must make shifts, as in this poem:

Uki fushi ya
takenoko to naru
hito no hate

Literally:

A sad confluence—
young bamboo shoots*
to become
everyone in the end

Revised version:

A sad confluence—
everyone in the end becomes
young bamboo shoots

In the end, what is any poem in translation except another blade of grass in the field—not a conclusion, but a provisional entryway into the vast ecology of the poem within its greater

*more literally, children of bamboo: *take no ko*

tradition? It is best to have two or three versions of any classic text in translation, one a strictly scholarly literal treatment, and another more imaginative, more interpretive translation, preferably by a sympathetic and knowledgeable poet.

But of course there can be no such thing as a literal translation since even individual nouns and verbs often have no exact equivalent from one language to another. Even when nouns and verbs do have reasonably exact equivalents, we still find problems of translation. When the Chinese or Japanese poet writes of "clouds and rain," he or she may mean literally "clouds and rain," or may mean sexual congress since "clouds and rain" has been a "pillow word" or fixed epithet for two millennia or more. In the hands of a good poet, the weather and the personal experience become interlocking parts of one compound metaphor. Since we don't have equivalent fixed epithets in English, we must learn to read the translation as well.

Horace was among the first to warn us against *verbo verbum* translation. Octavio Paz notes, "Every poem is a translation." The English language itself is a translation with roots in Greek, Latin and German, spiced by an admixture of foreign terminologies that have become Americanized through common usage.

My practice as a poet and as a translator is really one work evolving as much from my Zen practice as by any wish to "make" a poem. Translation has been for me a simultaneous learning and making. There are few stupidities I have not committed. But since I am *unsui*, a perpetual beginner in the temple of poetry and along the dharma path, I also understand that there is no perfect prescription, and that we are all students together. In the company of Chuang Tzu, Tu Fu, Li Po, Basho and Issa, the practice is refined, but perfection remains an illusive ideal rather than an attainable reality, and all translation a provisional conclusion.

When Basho advises his students, "Don't merely follow in the footsteps of the masters, but seek what they sought," I number myself among his students. I feel a solidarity with Tu Fu in his exile despite the fact that we are no longer living in a time of war, and despite the fact that I have been fortunate enough to have published more than thirty books, while he died an obscure poet. I translate because I want to be in their company—to comprehend their art, to learn what they learned and to be shaped by their learning, and because I want to make them available to others.

When an otherwise notable translator like Stephen Mitchell muddies the waters with something as irresponsible as his wild interpretation of Lao Tzu's *Tao Te Ching* passed off as translation, it is like a virus in a computer that begins to invade other programs. Mitchell writes that he felt no compunction to study the original Chinese because he somehow got the transmission directly from his Zen master, so felt free to interpret *Tao Te Ching* freely. In at least a couple of chapters, there is not as much as a single word brought over from the original. The problem with this kind of practice is that the naive reader might assume that the English bears some resemblance to the original, which all too often simply isn't so. Or as Chuang Tzu would say, "Not quite there yet, eh?"

To truly understand Lao Tzu, Chuang Tzu or most classical Chinese poetry, we would need a large scholarly apparatus to clarify all the allusions and explain a cast of characters and provide an explication of cultural-philosophical contexts and linguistic differences. We would know the *Analects* of Confucius and the *Classic of Filial Piety*, the *I Ching*, and elementary Chinese cosmology.

Bill Porter's translation of the *Tao Te Ching* is brilliant in part because it is accurate and in part because he includes insightful commentaries that previous translators have not known. Ursula LeGuin's recent translation sparkles with her own insightful commentary while remaining accurate translation.

Chuang Tzu to Tu Fu, Lu Chi to Bashō, the Taoist/Zen literary masters are the very foundation of my practice both as a poet and as a Zen Buddhist. When I say I "practice" the arts of poetry or translation, I mean to use the term as a doctor or lawyer "practices" his or her profession. Poetry in America is not a profession, but an avocation. Nevertheless, one is a practicing poet, a practicing Buddhist or Christian or Jew—or in my case Zen Buddhist atheist. (Buddhism itself is generally non-theistic.) I've always been moved by Gary Snyder's remark, "As a poet, I hold the most archaic values on earth." What Tu Fu valued, I value; what Bashō sought, I seek. The human condition remains relatively unchanged over a millennium or two. And I agree with Stanley Kunitz that poetry "has its source deep under the layers of a life, in the primordial self."

We are fortunate to live during the greatest time for poetry since the T'ang Dynasty. While academicians bemoan the decline of "the canon," the canon is expanding exponentially. One can't really begin to understand the East Asian canon without knowing Confucius, *The Lotus Sutra* (the foundation of Buddhism), Chuang Tzu, T'ao Ch'ien and the T'ang poets. Anyone who believes for a minute that Confucius is not as important as Plato is suffering severe tunnel vision. To understand something about Tu Fu and Bashō is to establish kinship in a great and powerful tradition.

American poetry has flowered precisely because we have brought these and many, many other masters into good American English. When I survey the great literary influences in our poetry of the last fifty years, I must include beside the many East Asians such poets as Rilke, Akhmatova, Rumi, Georg Trakl, Odysseus Elytis, George Seferis, Yannis Ritsos, Valéry, Neruda, García Lorca, Cavafy, Sappho, Paz, and dozens more. Their influences have provided sustenance and inspiration and models for forms and styles for hundreds of our poets. There are more terrific poets writing in America today than have lived here in the past two hundred years, and much of what they do, from surrealism to language poetry, sonneteering to "organic verse," is a direct or indirect result of the arts of translation.

Kunitz writes in his *Passing Through*: "Through the years I have found this gift of poetry to be life-sustaining, life-enhancing, and absolutely unpredictable. Does one live, therefore, for the sake of poetry? No, the reverse is true: poetry is for the sake of the life."

Over the years, in the midst of trying to figure out this or that poem, I have returned time and again to two thoughts. The first was Paul Hansen's advice twenty-five years ago as we huddled over a dictionary under kerosene light on his float-shack in the Skagit River. "Keep your crimes against the Chinese as few as possible." I know that I will never know as much as one-tenth of what Paul Hansen knows about Chinese language and poetry. I have benefited greatly from the works of great scholars and translators and from their personal generosity. Hard-nosed generosity is a fundamental aspect of classical Chinese poetry.

The second recurring thought is about the romantic myth that says Li Po died drunk on a boat crossing the Yellow River when he tried to embrace the moon on the water. There is nothing romantic or wonderful about getting things wrong. Perhaps my crossing of the great river will prove as foolish as master Li's. What is translated poetry, anyway, but a frail reflection of the moon dancing over dangerous waters?

I sit at the feet of the great old masters of my tradition not only to be in a position to pass on their many wonderful gifts, but to pay homage while in the very act of nourishing, sustaining and enhancing my own life.

> —Sam Hamill
> kage-an
> Spring, 4698
> Year of the Iron Dragon

Early Poetry

Festal Song

Against downed trees,
axes ring and ring,
and birds cry sharp—
one from the valley dark,
one from a standing tree—
voicing their common concern.
Look at that bird!
Bird it is, seeking its companion.
And a man?
Should he do less?
Kindred spirits respond to invitation:
that is "the good life."

Whew! Whew! they puff, cutting trees.
I strain wine until it clears.
The lambs are fatted.
Send for relatives and friends,
better something should detain them
than that I should not ask.
Tidy the courtyard.
Arrange eight overflowing dishes
of meats and grains
to seduce an educated palate.
Better something should detain them
than that I do not ask.

They fell and trim the hillside trees;
I strain abundant wine.
Dishes are arranged.
No one declines.

People's camaraderie can be tested
by serving dry provisions.
If I have wine, I strain it;
no wine, then I buy it.
Beat the drum,
lead us into the dance!
It's festival time!
We drink our finest spirits!

War Lament

Autumn flowers
are deep yellow when they fall.

Sorrows slice my heart,
leaving gaping wounds.

The flowers fall.
Only leaves remain.

Had I foreseen all this,
I'd have chosen not to be born:

sheep so thin their heads look huge,
fish traps catch nothing but the stars.

Some few men may eat,
but no one eats his fill.

War Lament

Every plant is burnt yellow
as we march by, day after day,
every man marching,
imprisoned by duty
in the four quarters of the State.

Every plant darkens,
every man wifeless, beyond pity.
On "punitive expedition,"
we are treated
as something less than human.

We aren't rhino or tigers
to be caged in desolation!
Pity our expedition—
dark of morning to dark night
there is no hope for respite.

We push our handcarts
slowly down the great roads,
but only small animals belong
in these deep wilds,
in this dark world.

Li Yen-nien (ca. 100 BCE)

Song

There's a beautiful woman in the north,
unrivaled in all this world.

One look from her, and a city of men succumbs;
another look conquers a country of men.

A woman whose beauty conquers cities and countries
will never be found again.

Lament

1.
The hills are white with snow
glinting under moonlight.

Remember this: I want you,
I want to see you before I go.

2.
We lived without benefit
of feast and vow and wine.

This morning, step down to the water
where the stream divides.

3.
Tears. Tears and tears.
What marriage is worth weeping over?

Oh, for one honest man!
We'd grow white-haired old together.

Ts'ao Ts'ao (155–220)

Drinking Song

Drinking, I sing of peace and of equality:

The tax collector knocks at no gate;
all rulers are virtuous and bright,
and their arms and legs, the ministers, are kind.

The people are well mannered, yielding without
quarreling,
foregoing litigation.

Three years' tilling makes nine years' provisions—
granaries overflow.
Our elders' backs are freed from loads.
Each fecund rain
contributes to the harvest.

Our fastest horses are withdrawn from war
to carry fertilizer.

Those who hold land or titles
show genuine affection for people,
promoting or demoting by merit,
attending like fathers or brothers.

Lawbreakers
receive a fitting punishment.
No one keeps what's found beside the road.
The prisons are all empty.
Midwinter courts have no criminals to try.

People of eighty or ninety
live out their lives quite naturally.

Great virtue impermeates it all—
even trees and plants and tiny things that crawl.

Lu Chi (261–303)

Song of Mount T'ai

Mount T'ai is one tall mountain rising,
rising into the courtyard of the heavens,

a rugged summit in the distance
lifting tiers of gloomy clouds.

These foothills have known the ritual sacrifice
of the emperor who built a pavilion.

This dark trail harbors many a ghost,
a hundred ancient spirits.

I prolong my song at the foot of Mount T'ai,
bravely singing my southern song.

Tzu Yeh (fourth century)

The Lotus Lover

A green lotus on waves of transparent blue:
the flowers grow red and new.

You want to collect these lovely flowers?
I'll give my lotus bud to you.

All Night

All the sleepless night
in the moon's white light,

alone. She listens.
Does his voice call out?

She replies to an empty room.

An End to Spring

Your leaving brought an end to spring;
longing burns through summer heat-waves.

Will I ever lift my dress for you again?
My pillow ever hold your lovely face?

Tzu Yeh (fourth century)

A Smile

In this house without walls on a hill,
the four winds touch our faces.

If they blow open your robe of gauze,
I'll try to hide my smile.

Illusions

Under bright moonlight,
night is endless,

the sleep I long for
never comes.

Suddenly I hear,
I think,

your voice.
And call for you,

my heart
racing into my throat.

Only an echo
answers,

only an echo
mocks me in the night.

An End to Spring

Spring has vanished,
leaving me heavy-hearted.

Now summer
threatens to grieve me more.

Why these silk curtains
beside my bed?

Will these two soft pillows
ever cradle our weary heads?

Late Spring

Willows bend to the sea breeze—
how suddenly time flies!

Magpies welcome the summer
while cicadas cry from the trees.

Bitter Harvest

Joyous, who can help but sing?
The one who is hungry eats.

I lean out the door at sunset:
bitter ones never forget.

Song

Longing, I watch out the open window,
my sash untied, long sleeves dragging.

This breeze lifts gauze so easily,
if my skirt should open, blame the warm spring wind.

Song

Winter skies are cold and low,
with harsh winds and freezing sleet.

But when we make love beneath our quilt,
we make three summer months of heat.

Tzu Yeh (fourth century)

Admonition

When she approached you on the street,
you couldn't possibly say no.

But your neglect
of me is nothing new.

Hinges soon sag on an empty door:
it won't fit snug like it did before.

Busy in the Spring

Bright moonlight shines through the trees.
In a rich brocade, the flowers bloom.

How can I not think of you—
alone, lonely, working at my loom.

T'ao Ch'ien (365–427)

Returning to My Fields and Gardens

When I was young, my world was disharmonious.
At root, fields and mountains were my nature.

Nevertheless, I lived in the dust of the world
for more than thirty years,

a caged bird longing for remembered groves,
a pond fish dreaming of deep seas.

Clearing brush along a southern trail:
living simply returns me to gardens and fields.

My three small acres hold
just a thatch-roofed hut

with willow and elm behind for eaves,
and peach and plum besides.

The memory of village life grows dim,
passing like smoke on gentle winds.

A dog barks down the road.
A cock crows in a mulberry tree.

I've swept the dust from my dooryard.
My empty room is a pleasure.

Thirty years locked in a cage,
but now I return to my own true nature.

Reply to Prefect Liu

You called me from lakes and hills,
but something made me waver:

good friends and family couldn't bear
to see me living elsewhere.

My heart recalled the good old days,
my home was a shack in the west.

The trail was overgrown; no one came.
There were a few old homes in ruins.

I repaired my roof with thatch
and prepared my fields for planting.

Fall winds turn this valley cold,
but spring wines remedy my hunger.

My daughter's not a son-and-heir,
but she provides my comfort.

Through months and years the busy world
grows more and more far distant.

Planting and weaving satisfy my needs.
What more should I require?

As the years of life march by,
all flesh and fame pass on together.

To My Cousin, Ching-yuan, Twelfth Month, 403

Hidden behind a rustic gate,
I sever my ties with the world.

Some days I look, but no one's there,
the old wooden gate stays closed.

Cold, the cold year-end winds,
snows cloaking everything.

Bending my ear, I hear nothing.
My eyes see only pure white,

winter air sharp as a blade up my sleeve.
Rice bowl and wine jug empty,

in the whole empty house
there is nothing to sustain me.

Reading the classics again,
sometimes I still find heroes,

old sages I dare not emulate,
but who stood strong in adversity.

I too will not choose the easy way.
My unemployment is not mere ineptitude.

My meaning lies beyond my words—
Who but you can understand my fate?

Passing Through Ch'ien-hsi, Third Month, 405

Months and years have flown
since I last traveled these hillside streams.

From dawn to dark I watch:
not a thing has changed.

Soft rain washes the trees,
bird on the rising breeze—

all things self-revealing,
all things interpenetrating.

Is this where I belong,
pressed to meet my duties?

My body may be subject
but my heart remains my own.

I dream all day of fields and meadows,
and long all day to return.

Lost, I long for a boat back home.
The cypress survives the frost.

Fire, Sixth Month, 408

At the end of a path, I built a thatch-roofed shack,
happy to avoid the flowered carriages of gentry.
But dry winds dogged the summer months—
my home in the woods was burned.

Without as much as a roof,
we make our home in a boat beside the gate.
The evening sky spreads wide wings.
The full moon rises high.

Our garden turns slowly green again,
but the birds have not returned.
I drift among a thousand thoughts,
watching the nine heavens.

Uncompromising since childhood,
now I find forty years have quickly passed.
My body slowly changes, but my heart remains intact,
keeping to an inner path stronger than diamond or jade.

Once, I'm told, grain was stored in the field
and all people filled their bellies,
content to rise at dawn
and return at dusk to sleep.

Those times are not my time.
I return to watering my garden.

Lament

The ways of heaven are mysterious,
the spirits pose a problem.

Since childhood, I struggled to do right—
forty-four years of struggle.

Things went bad when I was twenty.
At thirty, I lost my wife.

Fires burned my houses down
and weevils ate my grain.

Winds and rain ruined everything:
I couldn't fill a mouth.

In summer, we went hungry;
in winter we all slept cold.

Evenings, we longed for the cock crow;
at dawn, we chased away the crows.

It's my own poor karma, not heaven,
that leaves me troubled and bitter.

A name unearned, left for all the ages,
means no more to me than mist.

Drinking Alone in the Rainy Season

Whatever lives must meet its end—
that is the way it has always been.

If Taoist immortals were once alive,
where are they today?

The old man who gave me wine
claimed it was the wine of the immortals.

One small cup and a thousand worries vanish;
two, and you'll even forget about Heaven.

But is heaven really so far away?
It is best to trust in the Tao.

A crane in the clouds has magic wings
to cross the earth in a moment.

It's been forty years of struggle
since I first became reclusive.

Now that my body is nearly dead,
my heart is pure. What more is there to say?

Hsieh Ling-yun (385–433)

Crossing the Mountain, I Follow
the Chin-chu River

Monkey cries accompany the dawn
while the valley remains darkened.

Clouds gather beneath the cliffs
while dew still glistens on the flowers.

The path winds along the mountainside,
a dangerous trail through the hills.

I wade across shallow rapids
and climb a ladder up a cliff.

Through every twisting bend,
I delight in boating downriver.

Pepperwort and duckweed float up.
Reeds and rushes overtake the shallows.

I fill my cup at a waterfall
and pick young leaves from branches.

Did I see a mountain hermit
in his leafy jacket and rabbit-skin belt?

I gather orchids, but cannot bind them.
Picking hemp, I think there's no one to open my heart.

A kindly heart's a pleasure,
but who can see what's hidden there?

This landscape liberates—once enlightened,
I see things go their own way.

Visiting Pai-an Pavilion

Beside this dike, I shake off the world's dust,
enjoying walks alone near my brushwood house.

A small stream gurgles down a rocky gorge.
Mountains rise beyond the trees,

kingfisher blue, almost beyond description,
but reminding me of the fisherman's simple life.

From a grassy bank, I listen
as springtime fills my heart.

Finches call and answer in the oaks.
Deer cry out, then return to munching weeds.

I remember men who knew a hundred sorrows,
and the gratitude they felt for gifts.

Joy and sorrow pass, each by each,
failure at one moment, happy success the next.

But not for me. I have chosen freedom
from the world's cares. I chose simplicity.

Climbing Stone Drum Mountain

A traveler endures countless tribulations,
one grief hard on the heels of another.

The long, difficult road home winds
along a river under impassable mountains.

Without a friend to share my company, and time
passing quickly, I began the climb alone.

With no one to share my pleasure,
I sought a melancholy view—

a vast expanse of plain on my left,
deep, sharp gorges on my right.

At sunset, the mountain stream was highest.
Mountaintops vanished in the mist.

White flag and ivy grew together
and duckweed was bursting into leaf.

I collected fragrant plants I won't forget
as I enjoy them during times alone.

No sign of a friend come to visit.
The world's indifferent to my loneliness.

Written on the Lake While Returning
to Stone Cliff Hermitage

Dawn to dusk, the weather constantly changed,
mountain and lake sometimes vibrant in sunlight,

bright sunlight that made me so happy
I forgot about going home.

Leaving the valley at daybreak,
I didn't disembark until dusk,

forest and gorge clothed in shadows,
sunset clouds melting into evening mist.

There were water chestnuts and lotus,
cattails and rushes growing thickly.

I had to push them aside to pass southward,
happy to be reaching my home in the east.

When the mind stops striving, the world's not a problem.
A constant heart won't waver from the truth.

A few words to nurture the living, to say:
follow this teaching if you want to know the way.

Hsieh T'iao (464–499)

Complaint Near the Jade Stairs

In the evening at the palace, she lowers her pearl screen.
Fireflies in the garden flit and pause.

This long night, stitching silk,
thinking of him, she believes will never end.

Hsiao Kang (503–551)

Watching a Lonely Wild Goose
at Nightfall

There are few stars north of the Milky Way.
One wild goose calls, "Where am I going?"

If he'd known he'd lose his flock,
he would have begun his journey alone.

Yu Hsin (513–581)

Bidding Farewell to Secretary Chou

On the thousand mile road through Yang Pass,
not a single man travels home:

only wild geese along the river
flying south since the beginning of autumn.

Anonymous (ca. 600)

Farewell Poem

The green, green willows hang,
    sweeping the ground.
Breezes lift catkins, sending them
    across the sky.

When all the branches are stripped
    and the blossoms blown away,
I ask these travelers whether
    they'll ever come home again.

Wang Fan-chih (590–660)

Drinking Alone

Everyone's born with an empty body,
everyone breathes the same.

We are born, live, and die,
and are born to die again.

But we remember nothing.
Is this all there is?

In time, even bread
turns to stone on the tongue.

Forget the living and the dead!
Time to get drunk alone.

Poem

When the rich pass proudly by
on big, smooth horses,

I feel foolish
riding my scrawny donkey.

I feel much better
when we overtake

a bundle of sticks
riding a bony man.

Wang Po (ca. 650–676)

In the Mountains

Unhappy at being delayed at the Yangtze,
I yearn to travel a thousand miles home.

And all during this blustery evening,
from mountain after mountain, yellow leaves are blown.

Wang Chih-huan (688–742)

View from Heron Tower

The white sun is hidden in the mountains.
The Yellow River empties into the sea.

Climb up one floor:
you'll see a hundred miles more.

Returning Late to Lu-men Shan

A lone temple bell tolls at dusk
when Fishtowners stumble to their boats.

Others walk the riverbank home.
My own boat moves toward Lu-men Mountain.

Soon, Lu-men moonlight spills through misty trees
and I come again to the old hermitage,

the path leading through pines, the brushwood door,
back again to solitude and silence.

Where a hermit lives,
there's no need for companions.

Spring Dreams

In spring, I dream through dawn,
but hear birds everywhere, singing.

O voice of all-night wind and rain,
do you count the petals that are falling?

Wang Ch'ang-ling (d. 756)

Silent at Her Window

Too young to have known the meaning of sorrow,
in her spring dress she climbs the tower chamber.

New leaves on all the willows wound her.
She sent him off to war for nothing but a title.

Poems of Li Po

The Great Bird

When the Great Bird soars,
his wingbeats rattle the world,

but even he cannot save himself—
he is broken in the sky.

Something of his essence
will linger through the ages.

He will catch his sleeve on a tree
at the very edge of the world.

If you who follow after
understand, you must pass it on.

With Confucius gone,
who will be left to mourn?

In Memory of Ho Chi-chen

People in his homeland thought him mad,
so Ho Chi-chen wandered with the winds.

When we first met in Ch'ang-an,
he dubbed me the "Banished Immortal."

He loved good talk and his cup,
who lies under bamboo and pine.

Through a veil of tears, I see
poor Ho, hocking his ring for wine.

Li Po (701–762)

On Dragon Hill

Drunk on Dragon Hill tonight,
that banished immortal, Great White,

turns among yellow flowers,
his smile spread wide

as his hat sails off on the wind
and he dances away in the moonlight.

Parting

We cross the river narrows
and continue deep into the land of Chu.

Soon the mountains drop onto a plain
the river crosses, flowing into Heaven.

The moon reflects the wide, blank sky;
clouds rise into terraces and towers.

Good-bye. You ride the waters of our home
though you sail ten thousand miles.

Saying Good-bye in a Ch'in-ling Wineshop

Spring winds perfume the shop
with heavy blooming catkins.

A girl from Wu pours wine
and encourages our drinking.

With friends from the city
I come to toast and say good-bye.

About to part, I point them toward
the great east-churning river.

Can any river possibly flow
beyond the love of friends?

Summer Days in the Mountains

Too lazy even to move a feather fan,
stripped naked in the deep green forest,

even my headband left on a stone wall somewhere,
I let the pine winds ruffle my hair.

Listening to a Flute on a Spring Night in Lo-yang

A few dark notes from a jade flute
disappear into the spring breezes of Lo-yang.

At midnight, hearing "Willow Breaking Song,"
is there a soul who does not think of home?

Longing for Someone

Longing for someone in Ch'ang-an—
crickets sing in the autumn near the golden well.

Frosty winds bring a chill.
My futon's the very color of cold.

The lamp has almost burned out,
and I am exhausted by longing.

I open the curtain to see the moon,
but my sighs are all in vain.

She who is lovely as all the flowers
remains beyond the distant clouds.

The heavens are deep blue, and endless.
Below, the lapping waves are pale.

This sky, like my journey, knows no end.
We bear up our suffering as we go.

Even dreams cannot cross over
the vast mountains that divide us.

And this eternal longing
can turn a heart to dust.

Drinking Wine with a Mountain Hermit

We sit together among
blossoming mountain flowers,

drinking cup after cup
until I'm so drunk

I grow drowsy.
You, old friend, must leave.

Come tomorrow, if you choose,
but don't forget your lute.

Taking Leave of a Friend

Green mountains rise to the north;
white water rolls past the eastern city.

Once it has been uprooted,
the tumbleweed travels forever.

Drifting clouds like a wanderer's mind;
sunset, like the heart of your old friend.

We turn, pause, look back and wave.
Even our ponies look back and whine.

Ancient Airs

I climb high to look out upon the world,
all heaven and earth so very wide,

an autumn cloak of frost on everything,
these strong cold winds promising winter.

There is glory in the east-flowing river,
our concerns are only tiny waves.

Even the white sun is swallowed by clouds,
and the clouds drift on without rest.

Common sparrows roost high in wu-t'ung trees
while phoenixes nest in brambles.

Nothing left but to ramble home again,
tapping my sword to the tune "Hard Traveling."

Farewell to Yin Shu

The moon rises over White Heron Island.
At dawn, we will say a last farewell.

Already skies grow lighter, sun behind
Green Dragon Hill pushing up through clouds.

This flowing river feels nothing.
Winds will fill sails that carry him away.

Silenced by sadness, we can only watch,
then lift our cups, honoring old vows.

Remembering East Mountain

It's been forever since I returned to walk
the trails of my East Mountain home.

How many roses bloomed alone,
white clouds gathered only to be blown?

Who lives there now and stays up late
to watch this bright moon go down?

Fall River Song

Along Fall River, gibbons cry all night,
and Yellow Mountain has long white hair.

Blue Creek will never flood
like the rivers of my home.

My heart sinks in the river,
drowns in the longing to go home.

Am I doomed to wander forever?
These tears will swamp my boat.

Fall River Song

On Old River Mountain
a huge boulder swept clean
by the blue winds of heaven

where they have written
in an alphabet of moss
an ancient song.

At Ch'ang-men Palace

This palace was once magnificent,
but now inside there's only one old woman

who doesn't know spring from autumn
in a palace built of gold.

Heavy with dust, no one cleans it now.
The only visitor at night

is this huge lonely moon
tracing the walls with its fingers.

Questions Answered

You ask why I live
alone in the mountain forest,

and I smile and am silent
until even my soul grows quiet.

The peach trees blossom.
The water continues to flow.

I live in the other world,
one that lies beyond the human.

Mountain Drinking Song

To drown the ancient sorrows,
we drank a hundred jugs of wine

there in beautiful moonlight. We couldn't
go to bed with the moon so bright.

Then finally the wine overcame us
and we lay down on the empty mountain:

earth for a pillow
and a blanket made of heaven.

Saying Good-bye to Meng Hao-jan at Yellow Crane Pavilion

You said good-bye at Yellow Crane Pavilion
and sailed west, down into the valley
through the flowers and mists of spring
until your lonely sail vanished
in the blue sky's horizon,

and I was left watching the river
flowing gently into heaven.

To a Friend

Late autumn strips the distant hills
beyond the city gate.

A huge white cloud interrupts my dreams
and returns me to this world.

And you, old friend?
Flown silent as a crane.

Will you ever return
to your old home again?

In a Village by the River

The rain stops falling in this river village.
And now, the wine gone, you say good-bye.

Comfortable in your little boat,
you ride sails homeward on the water,

passing islands burning up with flowers,
passing slender river willows.

And what of the one you leave behind?
I return to my rock and my fishing line.

Drinking Alone with the Moon

I take my wine jug out among flowers
to drink alone, without friends.

I raise my cup to entice the moon.
That, and my shadow, make us three.

But the moon doesn't drink,
and my shadow follows silently.

Still, shadow and moon for companions,
I travel to the ends of spring.

When I sing, the moon dances.
When I dance, my shadow dances too.

Sober, we share life's joys;
drunk, each goes a separate way.

Constant companions although we wander,
we'll meet again in the Milky Way.

Return of the Banished

You return on currents and tides
after years in the wilds of the east.

How many are the sorrows of exile?
More than pearls in the seas.

About Tu Fu

I met Tu Fu on a mountaintop
in August when the sun was hot.

Under the shade of his big straw hat
his face was sad—

in the years since we'd last parted
he'd grown wan, exhausted.

Poor old Tu Fu, I thought then,
he must be agonizing over poetry again.

Going to Visit a Taoist Recluse on Heaven's Mountain Only to Find Him Gone

Dogs bark where the river sings,
and peach blossoms grow heavy with rain.

Deer wander through woods so deep
I cannot hear the noon-bell near the river.

Bamboo grows thick in blue-green mists
when the river plunges from the summit.

No one here to tell me where you've gone,
I linger, pining in the forest.

To the Tune: Beautiful Barbarian

Smoky mist weaves through cold mountain forests
leaving only a belt of heartrending green.

Twilight covers the tower
where I grieve alone in Jade Pavilion.

All the birds hurry home.
But how shall I find a way?

Long respite, brief respite,
traveling hard, day by day.

Li Po (701–762)

Seeing Off a Friend

Yesterday has flown, leaving only its sorrows.
That and the sorrows of today fill my heart with longing.
Autumn geese vanish in the wind.

I watch with my cup from the tower, thinking:
the old formal poets, the new who write in a casual way—
how they all love high-minded ideals.

Wanting to touch Heaven, they embrace the moon.
Drawing my sword to cut water, the water flows;
filling my cup to drown sorrow, the sorrows all return.

This life, this world, is struggle.
You'll let down your hair
and take to your boat tomorrow.

O-mei Mountain Moon

Tonight a half-moon
rises over O-mei,

its pale light
floating on the river.

Leaving Ching-chi, the river plunges
through Yangtze gorges.

I sail on to Yu-chow,
thinking of you all the way.

Crows at Dusk

In the yellow-cloud dusk, the crows
return to their nests near the city wall,
and as they settle, they call.

Alone at her loom in Ch'ang-an,
a girl weaves beautiful brocade.
But for whom?

Behind her gauze curtain,
she mutters as she works,
and when her shuttle finally stops,

she sulks, recalling her lover again.
She lies alone in bed all night.
And her poor tears rain.

Waterfall at Lu-shan

Sunlight steams the river stones.
From high above, the river steadily plunges—

three thousand feet of sparkling water—
the Milky Way pouring down from Heaven.

Old Style Poem

I climbed Lotus Mountain in the west
to see in the distance a bright star-girl
whose pale hand held a lotus.
She stepped from emptiness to emptiness,
her skirts a belted rainbow
sashaying in the breeze that bore her up
into the heavens, and from there she called
to me to climb to her cloud terrace,
and salute the immortals. Stunned,
I stood stark still and watched
her ride a swan into purple darkness.

I looked down only then on the Lo-yang River:
teeming with Tartar troops,
meadows rivered with blood,
wolves and jackals wear the caps of men.

Rising Drunk on a Spring Day

This world's a dream, so why
a lifetime of suffering?

I end the day ruinously drunk,
asleep on the porch till I wake confused.

An oriole explores the flowers,
and I ask, "Say, friend,

what season is it now?"
and it sings of spring breezes.

Moved almost to tears,
I lie down again with my wine

to compose a bright moon song,
but the feeling's gone before the song is done.

Complaint near the Jade Steps

Dew whitens the jade steps.
This late, it soaks her gauze stockings.

She lowers her crystal blind to watch
the breaking, glass-clear moon of autumn.

Quiet Night Thoughts

A pool of moonlight on my bed this late hour
like a blanket of frost on the world.

I lift my eyes to a bright mountain moon.
Resigned, remembering my home, I bow.

Listening to a Flute in Yellow Crane Pavilion

I came here as a wanderer
    thinking of home,
remembering my faraway Ch'ang-an.

And then, from deep in Yellow Crane Pavilion,
    I heard a beautiful bamboo flute
play "Falling Plum Blossoms."

It was late summer in a city by a river.

Looking for Master Yung Ts'un near His Hermitage

You live where green mountains reach almost
to the sky, indifferent toward the passing years.

Here where the old road disappears into
drifting clouds, I linger awhile by the river.

Dark oxen lie among the wildflowers;
high in pines, white cranes silently doze.

As I walk, twilight falls on the river and I
return alone, down through mist and cold.

Old Dust

We live our lives as wanderers
until, dead, we finally come home.

One quick trip between heaven and earth,
then the dust of ten thousand generations.

The Moon Rabbit mixes elixirs for nothing.
The Tree of Long Life is kindling.

Dead, our white bones lie silent
when pine trees lean toward spring.

Remembering, I sigh; looking ahead, I sigh once more:
This life is mist. What fame? What glory?

Women of Yueh

1.
The woman from Ch'ang-kan
has eyes more beautiful than the moon,

bare feet white as frost
without the stockings of the upper crust.

2.
Southern women have alabaster skin,
and this one steers her boat for play.

Springtime dances in her eyes
when she picks water lilies
to give to romantic passersby.

3.
Gathering lotuses by Yeh River,
she sings whenever someone passes,

then quickly hides her boat among the lilies—
so coy, pretending shyness.

4.
Mirror Lake's waters are moon-clear,
and the woman from Yeh River

has a face pale as snow
that trembles in the ripples.

Blue Water

He drifts on blue water under a clear moon,
picking white lilies on South Lake.

Every lotus blossom speaks of love
until his heart will break.

To Tu Fu from Shantung

You ask how I spend my time:
I nestle against a tree trunk,

listening to autumn winds
in the pines all day and night.

Shantung wine can't get me drunk.
The local poets bore me.

My thoughts head south with you,
like the river, endlessly flowing.

Springtime South of the Yangtze

The time of green spring winds returns.
The orioles will not stop singing.

My hair grows white on the banks of the Yangtze,
my home far beyond the mountains.

My heart soars with the clouds of Chin
while the moon casts my shadow in Chu.

Having squandered my life,
my garden is buried in weeds.

This late—so many years gone by—
nothing left but to sing alone

beyond the imperial gate.

Remembering Ancient Days in Yueh

When the king of Yueh returned
        after defeating the barbarians,
those who survived came home
        wearing embroidered clothes.
Court ladies lit the spring palace
        with the colors of flowers.
Nothing remains of them now
        but a few partridges flying there.

Zazen on Ching-t'ing Mountain

The birds have vanished down the sky.
Now the last cloud drains away.

We sit together, the mountain and me,
until only the mountain remains.

Poems of Wang Wei

Birdsong Valley

I lie at ease where cassia blossoms fall.
The night is still, the spring mountain empty.

The rising full moon surprises mountain birds:
they sing loudly in the spring valley.

Visiting the Mountain Hermitage
of a Monk at Gan-hua Monastery

He waits at dusk, bamboo walking stick in hand,
at the headwaters of Tiger Creek,
leading us on as we listen to mountain echoes,
following the water's way.

Patches of wildflowers bloom.
A solitary bird calls from the valley floor.
We sit evening zazen in the empty forest:
quiet pine winds bring the odor of autumn.

Sitting Alone on an Autumn Night

Sitting alone in the empty hall
late at night, I remember other temples.
Fruit ripens and falls in the mountain rain.
Insects call in the lamplit grass.

Nothing can be done about my whitening hair.
No alchemy produces yellow gold.
Struggling against inevitably growing old,
one can turn only to the dharma.

Mourning for Yin Yao

How long can one man live
before returning to emptiness?
I know you welcomed death.
Ten thousand things can trouble a heart.

Your good mother not yet buried,
your daughter is barely ten.
I hear from beyond the frozen wilderness
the desolate sounds of laments.

Clouds float across the empty sky.
A bird on the wing cannot sing.
Loneliness is the way of the wanderer.
The white sun soon grows cold.

I'm sorry that when you lived
and begged to study the dharma with me,
my teaching came too late
to bring you much success.

Old friends always have gifts to bring,
but in your lifetime, mine came a bit too late.
I failed you in many ways.
Tearfully, I close my brushwood gate.

At Li's Mountain Hermitage

The privileged fill the imperial ranks
while the commoner happily withdraws.
I follow the old hermit to his retreat
on the mountain high above the forest.

Wildflowers have yet to bloom.
Old trees and young penetrate the clouds.
Through bright daylight, he still sleeps,
even as mountain birds sing on.

Chi River Gardens and Fields

A solitary life beside Chi River.
Eastern winds sweep where no mountains lie.

The sun hides in the mulberry grove.
The river shines, winding beside the village.

Shepherds look back longingly at distant homes.
Dogs follow the hunters home.

What's a man of peace to do all day?
His brushwood gate stays closed.

Wang Wei (701–761)

Deer Park

No sign of men on the empty mountain,
only faint echoes from below.

Refracted light enters the forest,
shining through green moss above.

At Lake Yi

Flutes echo from the far shore
as we pause at sunset to bid farewell.

Green mountains, inverted on the lake,
plunge through pure white clouds.

The Way to the Temple

Searching for Gathered Fragrance Temple:
miles of mountains rise into clouds,
ancient trees darken the narrow trail.
Where is that mountain temple bell?

Snowmelt crashes down on boulders,
the sun grows cold in the pines before
it drowns in the lake. Keep your karma
in good working order: many dragons lie in wait.

Crossing the Yellow River

A little boat on the great river
whose waves reach the end of the sky—

suddenly a great city, ten thousand
houses dividing sky from wave.

Between the towns there are
hemp and mulberry trees in the wilds.

Look back on the old country:
wide waters; clouds; and rising mist.

Sailing Down the Han

Three rivers join in the wilds of Chu;
at Ching-men, nine flow through.

This river flows beyond earth and heaven,
mountains disappear in the void.

Rippling waves search for the sky.
Farther on, great cities line the bank.

Let's pause and enjoy this scenery.
Let an old mountain sage get drunk.

Wang Wei (701–761)

Reply to a Magistrate

Late in life, I care for ease alone—
to hell with official concerns.

Look! I make no plans for the future
but to go back to my forest home again.

Let pine winds loosen my robes,
mountain moons play my lute.

You want to taste success or failure?
A lone fisherman sings out on the water.

At a House in the Bamboo Grove

I sit alone in the bamboo dark
whistling and playing my zither.

And the woodsmen do not understand
how this bright moon chose me to shine on!

Return to Wang River

In the gorge where bells resound,
there are few fishermen or woodsmen.

Before I know it, dusk closes the mountains.
Alone, I return again to white clouds

and trembling water chestnuts
where willow catkins fly.

Spring grass colors the eastern landscape.
Snared in a web of grief, I close my wooden door.

At the Hermitage of Master Fu

The path winds through secret peaks and valleys,
through cloudy forests to the Dharma Hall.

Winged immortals play fine music.
Diligent nuns light incense.

Beyond the bamboo grove, mountains shine;
in deep shade, the pool remains cool.

How long has he sat in empty peace?
The pathway smells like spring.

Hermitage at Chung-nan Mountain

Growing older, I grow into the Tao:
now I make my home in southern mountains,

and go there on a whim to wander alone.
But even in all this splendor, things remain empty.

I climb to the headwaters
where clouds rise up from emptiness.

If I chance to meet another hermit in the woods,
we talk and laugh and never even think of home.

A Meal for the Monks

I came late to the dharma,
but each day, deepen my retreat.

Waiting for mountain monks,
I sweep my simple hut.

Then down from cloudy peaks
you come through knee-deep weeds.

We kneel on tatami, munching pine nuts.
We burn incense and study the Way.

Light the lamp at twilight:
a single chime begins the night.

In every solitude, deep joy.
This life abides.

How can you think of returning?
A lifetime is empty like the void.

Poems of Tu Fu

Sunset

How beautiful the river is in spring
with sunset filling the window.

The garden on the bank is sweet,
and so is the smoke of the boatmen.

Sparrows squabble in the branches,
insects buzz through my court.

Ah, heady unstrained wine—one cup
and a thousand griefs will vanish.

Random Pleasures (I)

A dragon sleeps three winter months,
the old crane longs to fly a thousand miles.

The ancients we admire
were as foolish as we are now.

Hsi K'ang died too young,
but K'ung-ming found one admirer.

They are like two hillside pines:
their use determines their worth.

In winter snow, their trunks impress,
but soon they, too, will fall.

Random Pleasures (II)

T'ao Ch'ien withdrew from all the world,
but he could not find the Way.

Reading through his poems now,
I find him always complaining.

He struggled all his life;
his gift did not come early.

His sons were wise or foolish,
but why should T'ao Ch'ien worry?

Rising Spring Waters

The river's up two feet overnight.
No way these banks can hold it.

Near the market, there are boats for sale.
If I had money, I could buy one

and moor it at my gate.

Evening near Serpent River

Breezes sigh, rising over bright tiled steps.
The round sun sinks below the wall.

Wild autumn geese slowly vanish
as sunset lengthens all the clouds.

Leaves have begun to drop already.
Cold flowers lose their fragrance.

I add my tears to the river.
At slack tide, only the moon is pure.

Descending Through Dragon Gate

The river drops from Dragon Gate
between walls of naked granite.

High winds kick up high waves
that have tossed ten thousand years.

The pathway veers and winds,
blown like a single thread.

This shaky bridge is hung
from hand-chipped nooks in rock.

My eyes float down like falling petals.
Misty rain whistles through my hair.

My whole life hangs in the balance:
one slip and it's all over.

I've heard of other fearsome trails,
and some I've had to try.

But whatever I think is dangerous
I'll measure against this climb.

Dragon Gate Gorge

Dragon Gate cuts a wide gorge.
Trees line the road from the city gate,

and the imperial palace is imposing.
The temples are silver and gold.

The seasons shift. I come and go;
the lands and waters roll on.

Of all those I met along this road,
will I ever meet any again?

Yen-chou City Wall Tower

I came east to pay a son's respects,
and now I look out from South Tower:

clouds reach from T'ai-shan to the eastern sea,
and a great plain covers Ch'ing and Hsu.

There was a monument to a tyrant on that peak,
and ruins lie where a kind prince ruled a city.

I have always valued antiquity.
Let others go on home. I will remain alone.

New Year's Eve at the Home of Tu Wei

Seeing the year end at my brother's home,
we sing and toast with pepper wine.

The stable is noisy with visitors' horses.
Crows abandon trees lit by torches.

Tomorrow morning I turn forty-one.
The slanting sunset shadows lengthen.

Why should one exercise self-restraint?
I may as well stay drunk all the days of my life.

Looking at Mount T'ai

T'ai-shan is a holy place, incomparable,
reflecting the green of the plains,

home of a thousand mysteries and more.
Dawn and dusk are born here in a moment.

Gathering clouds erase the unreal world.
Birds sail slowly out of sight.

Like Master Kung, I'll climb the summit
and watch all other mountains dwindle.

Leaving Ch'in-chou

The old monastery north of the city
was once a famous palace.

Now moss and lichen grow on the temple gate
and the red-green palace hall stands empty.

The moon is bright, the dew heavy,
and winds push clouds along the river.

Wei River flows steadily east without feeling.
I am alone with my sorrow.

Passing Mr. Sung's Old House

Mr. Sung's old house collapses.
The pond is full of moss.

I wandered here as a boy,
and was invited to leave a poem.

Old neighbors tell me stories now
until we lapse, at last, into silence.

The old oak looms like an aging general.
Sunset. Winds grieve its trembling leaves.

Visiting the Monastery at Lung-men

I explored the grounds with monks this evening,
and now the night has passed.

Heavy silence rises all around us
while late moonlight spills through the forest.

The mountain rises almost into heaven.
Sleeping in the clouds is cold.

A single stroke of the early prayer-bell wakes me.
Does it also waken my soul?

Going to the Palace with a Friend at Dawn

The water-clock marks dawn,
the peach blossoms rosy as wine.

Dragons and snakes on banners snap in the warm
        morning sun.
Sparrows and swallows glide on palace breezes.

I can smell the palace incense on your sleeve.
Poems should drip from your brush like pearls.

Who influences the court for more than one generation?
Another pheasant feather floats in the palace pool.

Taking Leave of Two Officials

At the Government Office Building,
wu-t'ung trees shade the empty courtyard.

Beaten by public office, you finally return home.
To stay or leave? Thinking breaks my springtime mood.

The palace walls will divide us
and clouds will bury the hills.

All men long for noble horses.
But don't let old age catch you unprepared.

To Li Po on a Spring Day

There's no poet quite like you, Li Po,
you live in my imagination.

You sing as sweet as Yui,
and still retain Pao's nobility.

Under spring skies north of the Wei,
you wander into the sunset

toward the village of Chiang-tung.
Tell me, will we ever again

buy another keg of wine
and argue over prosody and rhyme?

River Pavilion

I lie out flat on the river pavilion
reciting poems or dreaming.

Water roars by, but my heart grows still.
Clouds drift over and my mind responds as lazily.

Nothing moves in springtime dusk.
Such joy in the secret want of things.

How can I retire to my forest home again?
To dispel my melancholy, I write another poem.

Random Pleasures (III)

All day, all night, I worry,
wondering over my brother.

Alive or dead, I cannot know,
so many roads between us.

The rebels broke our lines, and we scattered.
Now we starve and freeze, looking for each other.

I long for the squeak of my farmhouse gate,
but fear the wolves and tigers may find me.

Each bird and beast has its place:
high up, cloudy, a single line of geese.

Random Pleasures (IV)

Blown by winds, the thistledown
drifts where it will, falling

through a thousand feet of frozen sky
to find another world.

The crooked path to my old home
has been deserted three long years.

Far off, the beacon flares blaze up—
chariots and weapons flood the eastern pass.

How long is one man's time on earth?
How long must the life of a wanderer last?

After Rain

At Heaven's Border, the autumn clouds are thin
and driven from the west by a thousand winds.

The world is beautiful at dawn after rain,
and the rains won't hurt the farmers.

Border willows grow kingfisher green,
the hills grow red with mountain pears.

A Tartar lament rises from the tower.
A single wild goose sails into the void.

The Draft Board at Shih-hao

As I was lodged at Shih-hao one night,
the draft board came for inductees.

While his wife delayed them at the gate,
one old man slipped over his wall and away.

Tu Fu (712–770)

The senior officer, in a rage,
cursed the woman into tears,

and then I heard her speak:
"All three of our sons went off to war.

And now a single letter returns—
two sons dead on the battlefield,

one on his last life's breath.
The dead are lost forever.

There's no one left at home
but a grandson nursing mother's breast,

too young to leave her side.
And she so poor her skirts are made of patches.

Although my strength has long since flown,
take *me* tonight, I beg you,

and I'll go to Ho-yang
and cook you all your breakfast."

The night and the voices passed,
except for the woman's sobbing.

I turned to the trail, first light breaking behind me
as the old man bid farewell to his family.

Song of the War Wagons

Wagons clang and horses cry
as soldiers pass with bows and arrows.
Families clamor to watch them go.
A huge cloud of dust swallows the trembling bridge.
Clinging to their clothes, they weep and stumble by,
their cries echoing through the sky.

And if you questioned them, they would say,
"Conscripted at fifteen, we fought for the north;
now almost forty, we move to fight in the west.
Once, villagers gave us honors.
Now we return white-haired, heading toward frontiers.
We've shed a sea of blood.
Still the emperor wants more.
East of the mountains, a thousand villages,
ten thousand villages, turn to bitter weeds.
Even when strong women work the fields,
our canals and crops are feeble.
The warriors of Ch'in fight on,
driven like dogs and cattle.

You may ask, but we don't dare complain.
This winter we await new troops
while officials raise new taxes.
But where will the money come from?
We've learned the grief of raising sons—
not like the quiet joy of daughters
we can marry to our neighbors."
Our boys lie under the weeds.
Near Kokonor, their old white bones
remain with no one to collect them.
Old ghosts and new complaints: you can hear them
all night long through falling mist and rain.

To Li Po on a Winter Day

Alone in my secluded hut,
I think of you all day, Li Po.

Whenever I read of friendship,
I remember your friendly poems.

Harsh winds tatter your old clothes
as you search for the wine of endless life.

Unable to go with you, I remember only
that old hermitage we'd hoped to make a home.

Moon on the Cold Food Festival

Homeless on Cold Food Festival Day,
I have nothing but this river of my tears.

If I cut down the moon's one cassia tree,
wouldn't the moonlight be brighter?

When red flowers bloom for lonely lovers,
her brow will be knit by sorrows.

No complaints. Like Cowboy and Weaving Girl,
we'll cross the river in autumn.

Moonlit Night

This same moon hangs over Fu-chou.
Alone, she'll lean out her window to watch it.

Our poor children are too small
to even remember Chang-an.

Dew will dampen her perfumed hair.
Clear moonlight makes her bare arms cool.

Will we ever sit again in her window,
the tears finally gone from our faces?

Lament for Ch'en T'ao

The first month of winter the blood of ours sons
flowed like water through Ch'en T'ao Marsh.

The whole country empty, sky clear, quiet,
forty thousand died here on a single afternoon.

Barbarians return with arrows dipped in blood,
drunk in the streets, howling Barbarian songs.

We turn our eyes away and cry toward the north,
praying night and day the imperial army will come.

Word from My Brothers

Word arrives from far P'ing-yin—
my brothers are still alive.

They traveled hard to far villages
searching for supplies.

But even there, the fires of war
are blazing up again.

Fresh tears fall on the fallen:
infirmity, old age, . . .

how can I possibly know
whether I'll ever see them again?

Passing the Night

Flowers beside the palace fade,
the sun sinks into the hills.

Last birds sing their way back home
and the first stars faintly shimmer

over a thousand palace doors.
The moon is huge and round.

Awake in the night, I listen
for the tinkle of keys in locks

like jade bridle-bells
set ringing in the wind.

At my dawn audience, they'll ask,
"I trust your night was peaceful?"

Poem for Mr. Li in Early Spring

Though sick, I rise at dawn—
your poem, "Grief in Early Spring," has come.

It multiplies the autumns in my heart,
and I realize old age has found me.

Tender peach-buds all blush red
as the willow shoots turn green.

Night after night, I dream of time, but
within the Four Seas, only dust and wind.

Farewell Rhyme

Reluctant, I must take leave from war
to tend my ailing garden.

But before the journey, this poem of good-bye.
We'll lighten our sadness with wine.

Rain fell hard all through the fall,
and now the weather is clearing.

Climbing mountain trails, I'll hear bugles everywhere,
but how will I bear their calling?

P'eng-ya Road

I remember fleeing the rebels
through dangerous northern canyons,

the midnight moon shining bright
on narrow P'eng-ya Road.

So poor we went on foot,
we were embarrassed meeting strangers.

A few birds sang in the valleys,
but we met no one returning.

My daughter was so starved she bit me,
she screamed her painful hunger.

I clamped her mouth shut tight,
fearful of wolves and tigers.

She struggled hard against me,
she cried and cried.

My son was sympathetic
and searched the wilds for food.

Then five days of heavy rain arrived,
and we trudged through freezing mud.

We had no coats, no shelter,
we were dressed in cold, wet clothes.

Struggling, struggling, we made
but a mile or two each day.

We ate wild fruits and berries,
and branches made our roof.

Mornings we slogged through water;
evenings we searched for skyline smoke.

We stopped at a marsh
to prepare our climb to the pass,

and met a Mr. Sun
whose standards are high as clouds.

We came through the dark
and lamps were lit, gates opening before us.

Servants brought warm water
so we could bathe our aching feet.

They hung paper banners
in our honor.

Mrs. Sun came out with all her children.
They wept for our condition.

My children slept, exhausted,
until we roused them with food.

Our host took a vow
he'd always remain my brother.

His home was made our home,
to provide for every comfort.

Who could imagine in such troubled times
he'd bare his heart and soul?

A year has passed since that fated night.
The Barbarians still wage war.

If I had the wings of the wild goose,
I'd fly to be at his side.

The Journey North

On the first day, eighth moon,
autumn in our lord's second year,

I travel north searching for my family,
inquiring everywhere under this blue, blank sky.

Welcomed at court or cast out, no man
these days has time for leisure.

Humbled by imperial favor, I return by decree
to my poor thatched hut in the mountains.

Signing out at the palace gate, I linger,
overcome with fears and doubts—

I always seem to fall short of my mark—
I can't ignore my duty to my lord.

Our lord has made a renaissance:
he is compassionate and just.

To the east, Barbarians still rebel.
I am torn between my duties.

Tearful, I long for Traveling Palace.
My journey begins in confusion.

The whole world is walking wounded,
but the savagery continues.

I make my slow, lonely way across
a devastated land—not even smoke

from a fire—and the few I meet are casualties,
wounds bleeding. They groan and they weep.

Turning toward Feng-hsiang,
camp banners flutter in faint light.

I climb the cold trail into mountains,
crossing endless empty campgrounds.

The Pin-chou Plain sinks below,
Ching River rolling on and on.

A wild tiger springs before me:
his roar could shatter granite.

Wild autumn flowers wilt.
Wagon ruts scar the road.

Climbing into clouds, my spirits rise.
Here is contemplation, here is solace.

There are chestnuts and acorns
and wild berries everywhere,

some as red as cinnabar,
some as black as lacquer.

They have rain and dew from heaven
and grow sweet or tart by nature.

Homesick for Peach Blossom Spring,
I regret my tribulations even more.

From this high trail, I see the Fu-chou hills,
and canyons and mountains beyond them.

My servant high behind me in the trees,
I rush down to meet the river.

Owls cry in the mulberry trees,
the field mice ready for winter.

We cross the battleground at midnight:
cold moonlight falls on frozen bones.

Ten thousand men enlisted at T'ung-kuan,
now ten thousand men are gone.

Who destroyed the clans of Ch'in,
who murdered half our men?

When I dreamed I fell in Barbarian dust,
it turned my dark hair white.

It's taken a year to reach my hut
and find my poor wife in rags.

Seeing me, she cries like wind through pines
and weeps a stream of tears.

My boy who brightened my life
is pale as winter snow.

He turns to hide his tears.
His bare feet scuff the dust.

My girls stand by the bed in tatters,
their dresses barely reaching to their knees.

Ocean waves embroidered on my old robe
were cut into mismatched patches,

sea-dragon and purple phoenix severed
to repair their shabby clothes.

A poor scholar, I agonize,
and lie three days in bed and vomit.

My bag holds one small blanket—
I can't even warm my family.

I unwrap a little rouge and powder,
and then unfold the blanket.

My poor wife's face slowly brightens
and my girls brush out their hair,

giggling, imitating their mother,
rouge splotched on cheeks,

powder in their eyes and hair,
eyebrows painted crooked.

It makes this poverty almost enough,
returning home alive.

They question, tugging my beard for attention,
and I haven't the heart to stop them.

I tolerate rough, noisy children,
remembering the grief of war.

Finally reunited, at last I can console them,
but how can I support them?

Even our lord must eat the dust of exile.
Who knows when the killing will end?

I search the skies for a sign
and all the heavens shudder.

Cold winds howl from the north,
along the Uighur trails,

delaying the day we'll be rescued
by the Uighur charge to the front.

The Uighurs number five thousand troops,
ten thousand horses before them.

They don't require great numbers,
preferring surprise attack.

Quietly vicious like circling hawks,
they're quicker than well-placed arrows.

After debate and confusion,
our lord has chosen to trust them.

Soon, we'll regain Lo-yang,
then the capital at Ch'ang-an.

The imperial army marches east
to set a major ambush.

Recapturing both towns,
they'll also retake the mountains.

Winter darkens the heavens.
This is death's long season.

The year will judge the Barbarians,
the months will crush the Tartars.

Since they cannot escape their fate,
our best years lie ahead.

We endured the evil princes of antiquity
and of the recent past;

we quartered vile officials
and exiled their hired thugs;

Hsia and Yin were ended
at the hands of evil women;

Chou and Han were wounded,
but lived to rise again.

Praise our General Ch'en—
he inspires as he leads.

Through him, we'll have a second life;
without him, our nation might have perished.

The Great Hall waits, empty and cold;
no one lingers at the gate.

But soon we'll regain lost splendor
as our lord names a golden court.

Sent to the Magistrate of P'eng-chou

A hundred years, and half have passed already.
Autumn arrives with its cold and hunger.

I wonder after the Prefect of P'eng-chou: when
will I be rescued from all my present hardships?

Leaving Government Offices

It is spring, almost dawn when the crowds gather
near the court with all their banners.

Flowers drop their petals as I retire from court.
Willows open their leaves.

Snowmelt dampens the walls.
Clouds cover the palace, darkening the halls.

Alone, in secret, I burn my draft memorial.
In my saddle, I yearn for a rooster's perch.

Another Spring

In all the country,
only the landscape is firm.
It is springtime in the city.
Weeds cover everything:

trees are overgrown,
flowers watered only with our tears.
Even the birds have learned to moan.

The war's beacon fires
have lit the hills for months.
I'd give anything for a letter.
I scratch my poor white head
and hair falls out,
and my hair's already so thin
it can barely hold a hairpin.

Drinking at Crooked River

Beyond the park, at River's Head,
the water's calm, the palace disappears.

Peach and willow blossoms scatter
as orioles fly up together.

Drinking, I don't care what they say—
I never cared for the court.

From my office I now see the immortals
have long since sunk into the sea.

Old and grieved, I see it's futile
to lament the duties I evaded.

Crooked River Meditation

Each falling petal diminishes spring.
Ten thousand of them sadden me.

Spring flowers pale, and I grieve,
and ease my remorse with wine.

Kingfishers nest in the temple hall.
A stone unicorn adorns a royal grave.

Taking my pleasures where I find them,
I fill my cup again.

Drinking with Elder Cheng the Eighth at Crooked River

At River's Head, birds swarm through willow flowers.
Marsh birds and wild ducks commingle.

But spring holds nothing for two old men,
just our wine jar and remembrance.

Those beside the emperor can't find a place of their own.
How can this old body no longer have a home?

You are still a tower of strength. How could you
even think of planting melon seeds beside a mansion gate?

To Abbot Min the Compassionate

Has it really been thirty years?
Writing this, I can't choke back the tears.

Are you still the servant of culture?
And who can an old man sing to?

Who packs your heavy Go board up the hill?
I remember your robe as our boat drifted on the water.

Now, they say, I've a future in office.
Me, a white old head dozing, drinking, dozing off again.

Dreaming of Li Po

1.
Parted by death, we'd strangle on our tears;
parting in life, we've memories to cling to.

There is pestilence south of the river,
you are exiled, and I have not a word.

Old friend, I see you only in dreams,
but you know my heart is with you.

It's not the same as having your living spirit:
that road's too long to be measured.

Your spirit is in the heart of green maple,
your spirit returns to the dark frontier.

Tu Fu (712–770)

Tangled in the nets of law, tell me,
how can the spirit soar?

Moonlight fills my room. Your poor face
shines, reflected in the rafters.

The waters are deep, the waves wide.
May peaceful serpents pass you by.

2.
All day, huge clouds roll by.
You, exile, must travel.

Three nights I dreamed of you,
I dreamed we were together.

"I try, I try," you say, "but
this bitter road is difficult to travel:

winds drive lakes and rivers into waves,
my boat and oars would fail."

Leaving, you smoothed your long white hair
like a man who embraced his failures.

In Ch'ang-an, they lavish praise on bureaucrats
while you endure and endure.

They say that heaven's net is wide.
We're tangled in the web of aging.

Your fame will last ten thousand years
though you are silent, vanished from this world.

Heavenly River

Heavenly River is muddy year-round,
except in the clarity of autumn

when a few small clouds make shadows.
But it's always bright at night.

Stars that swim the river shine on the capitol dome.
The river carries off the moon to set beyond the border.

Altair and Vega cross the river each autumn,
and neither wind nor wave can stop them.

Thinking of Li Po

A cold wind out of the wilderness.
What would you recommend?

When will the wild goose bring news
from the Lakes-and-Rivers land?

Poets must live without success,
driven on by daemons.

Remember the ghost of poor Ch'u Yuan—
send him a poem down the river.

Watching the Distances

I watch the limitless distance of autumn,
the far-off dark rising up in layers

where icy waters merge with the frozen sky
and the city is blurred with mist.

Last leaves are torn into flight by winds,
and sunless, distant peaks fade fast.

A lone crane flops home at dusk.
The trees are full of crows.

Ch'iang Village

Western clouds, hill above hill,
vermilion poured over the sunset,
and the sun walks into the earth.
Birds sing everywhere at my hermitage
as I return, suddenly old and weary.

It's a wonder I survive.
My wife and children weep.
The winds have blown me away
and waves have washed me back.
I'm lucky to be alive.

Neighbors swarm over our wall
sighing, crying and shouting.
Red-eyed with our tears,
we light the evening candle—
together we enter the dream.

The Cricket

The cricket is so small a thing,
yet moves us with tender chirping—

so quiet out among the weeds,
now it's crept under our bed to sing.

Its song brings an aging pilgrim tears,
it keeps the lonely wife awake.

Neither guitar nor flute can sing
as sweetly as natural music.

Listless

I can't bear a journey to the village—
I'm too contented here.
I call my son to close the wooden gate.

Thick wine drunk in quiet woods, green moss,
jade-gray water under April winds—
and beyond: the simmering dusk of the wild.

Firefly

You who are born in decay
dare not fly into the sun.

Too dim to light a page,
you spot my favorite robe.

Wind-tossed, you're faint beyond the curtain.
After rain, you're sparks inside the forest.

Caught in winter's heavy frost,
where can you hide, how will you resist it?

Sick Horse

Old horse, I've pushed you hard
through frontier snow and ice.

Now the autumn dust exhausts you,
you grow old and stubborn and sick.

You were never much to brag about,
but you kept your spirits high.

Now you suffer your last humility,
and all I can do is sigh.

Empty Purse

Tasted, the green cypress is bitter.
But morning clouds can be eaten.

My generation sold itself for money,
but my way has not been easy:

a cold stove, a well of solid ice each morning,
thin clothes and a cold bed at night.

My empty purse is embarrassed.
I leave it my last thin penny.

Departing from Ch'in-chou

As old age weakens me, I grow lazy and foolish.
I make no plans for the future.
Hungry, I remember a land of plenty;
cold, I recall the warmth of the south.
In early November, Han-yuan
is cool and crisp like autumn,
but leaves have not turned yellow and fallen,
and the landscape still is lovely.
Chestnut Station promises good fortune,
and the plains are thick with farms
growing delectable yams
and wild honey and forests of bamboo shoots.
There are shimmering ponds for fishing.
Although my wanderings have grieved me,
this journey restores my country spirit.

But so many people pass through Ch'in-chou,
I fear I'll become entangled—
appalling social functions
and touring won't assuage my worries.
Ominous boulders shadow these ravines,
and these sandy farms grow smaller.
How can I possibly linger
where nothing brings an old man peace?
The lonely lookout was swallowed by the dark.
Ravens cry from the city walls.
We depart at night in our carts, our horses
pausing to drink at ponds.
The moon and stars rise clear
above the mist and clouds,
reaching the endless void of space.
The way goes on forever.

Impromptu

We descend on horses onto the battleground.
The emptiness is wide.

Winds moan in the clouds,
yellow leaves blow by my feet.

On anthills among tangled grasses
lie a thousand shattered bones.

Passing by, old folks can only sigh,
while the young want another front.

Between the Han and the Huns,
alternate wins and losses:

the frontier's never secure.
How can anyone hope to find

a good general so our armies
can enjoy a quiet night of sleep?

Song of T'ung-ku

Already old, and still without a name,
I've starved three years in these mountains.

The ministers of Ch'ang-an all are young,
their money and honors earned.

My friends, the mountain sages,
dwell only on the past, in their hurting.

I chant this last song sadly, my eyes
on the August sky where the white sun races.

Becoming a Farmer

Brocade City lies in dust and smoke.
This river village has only a dozen houses.

Lotuses spread their leaves and float.
Good wheat bends from its weight.

Here, far from the capital,
I will farm till I am old.

Ko Hung sought immortality in cinnabar,
but here I will meet my fate.

The Servant Boy Delivers

The pears are green as new jade;
plums and apricots slowly grow yellow.

My boy comes quietly to the garden
bearing his basket of fruit.

Soft winds bring a heady fragrance.
The plums still drip with dew.

All for this lazy guest of rivers and lakes
as long days lengthen into years.

In a Village by the River

The clear river curves around our village:
these long summer days are beautiful, indeed.

Swallows swoop from the eaves,
the gulls all flock to the water.

My wife draws a rice-paper Go board
while our sons bend fishhooks from needles.

This medicine is all a sick man needs.
What man could ask for more?

Early Rising

Now that spring's returned, I like to get up early.
Reclusive living soothes the tattered soul.

Replace the stones of a caved-in wall,
thin trees for a view of the mountains.

On hands and knees, I clear a trail,
hidden, snaking up a hill—

then see my servant boy returning:
cold wine in a huge clay jar.

To a Guest

Spring waters run north and south from here,
but we have only the gulls for guests.

Now you've climbed our bramble path
and entered our rough wood gate.

This far from town, our cooking isn't fancy.
Stale rice wine is all a poor man offers.

Sit here. I'll fetch my ancient neighbor
to come and help us drink it.

Homestead

My homestead lies beside a clear stream,
its wicker gate on an unused road.

Deep grass hides it from the marketplace.
It's so secluded, I don't even have to dress.

Branch by branch, the willows droop;
tree after tree, the loquats still smell sweet.

Sunset reflects the fishing cormorants
drying their beautiful black wings.

In Seclusion

It is evening before I rise.
Out of work, I find the house is peaceful.

Bamboo fences the wilds
and the water reflects my cottage.

My sons are lazy boors,
my wife complains of constant poverty.

I'd like to be drunk a hundred years.
It's already been a month since I even combed my hair.

The Madman

My house lies west of Thousand Mile Bridge
near Hundred Flower Creek

where this old recluse delights:
each green bamboo in the wind

trembles like a girl, each red blossom
of the lotus adds perfume.

Old friends have joined the bourgeoisie
and no longer write me letters.

My children grow pale as ghosts
from hunger. The Madman only laughs

before he drowns in the gutter—
growing older, I grow madder.

A Hundred Worries

Fourteen and still a boy,
I ran wild as a calf in spring.

When the pears were ripe in autumn,
I climbed a thousand trees a day.

Now my fiftieth year approaches,
I grow lazy—I nap when I should walk.

Polite when I visit friends,
a hundred worries plague me.

At home, the rooms remain empty
and my wife understands my grief.

Our children won't bow to their father,
but weep for food in the barren kitchen.

Random Pleasures (V)

Grieved, I idle and doze
while spring sneaks up the river.

So why these numberless blossoms,
why do the orioles sound bitter?

Random Pleasures (VI)

The peach and plum I planted were my own.
Though low, my walls still mark my garden.

Spring winds still come to plunder:
at night they steal my blossoms.

Random Pleasures (VII)

River swallows know my shack is humble:
they come and go at random.

Mud-nests in my scrolls, turds all over my lute,
they fly so close I can touch them!

Random Pleasures (VIII)

Unemployed and lazy, I wander around the village.
I leave my sons behind, beside the garden gate.

I take my rice to a mossy bed in the woods
to sleep out in the breeze that blows in from the lake.

Random Pleasures (IX)

West of my hut, I grow mulberry;
down by the river there is wheat.

How many times will I see spring turn into summer?
I cling to my honey-sweet rice wine.

Evening after Rain

Sudden rain this afternoon
saved my thirsty garden.

Now sunset steams the grass
and the river softly glistens.

Who'll organize my scattered books?
Tonight I'll fill and fill my glass.

I know they love to talk about me.
But no one faults me for my reclusive life.

Song for a Young General

Brocade threads and summer reeds
weave a tune of clouds and breezes.

How many times in one man's life
can he listen to heaven's music?

After Solstice

After solstice, the sunlight slowly lengthens. From
Two-Edged Sword Trail my thoughts return again to
        Lo-yang.

Neither my robe of office nor my big white horse
means anything at all—

nor would a valley of gold and bronze camels
when I am so far from home.

Plum blossoms? I don't see a thing.
Mountain cherry and sweet bloom severed,

one aches, longing for the other
like two separated brothers.

Sorrows weigh me down when poems
should touch the roots of joy to rouse it,

but with each poem completed,
chanting, the old, cold ache is started.

In Praise of Rain

We suffered drought, months without rain.
Then, this morning, clouds climbed from the river:

misty rain began to drizzle,
falling in every direction.

Birds returned to their nests,
forest flowers freshened all their colors.

Now, at dusk, the rains continue their song
and I want to hear it all night long.

Singing Girls (Written in Jest)

1.
Officials are quick to disembark,
welcomed by girls who greet the barges.
When these girls sing,
the river reflects their fans,
and when they dance,
their dresses touch the sand.
Their white sleeves luff in the wind,
wine jars bob in the waves.
How inviting as they compete with painted eyes,
rekindling youthful fires!

2.
Song and dance retired the blistering sun.
Now flute songs fill the sky.
Shining eyes dance a delicate chorus;
their headdresses sway in line.
Horses wait, rumps to the hills,
barges float a river of perfume.
Friend, your wife's at home alone:
stay away from wild ducks and drakes.

Clear after Rain

Long after rainfall, Sorceress Hills grow dark.
Now they brighten, stitched with gold and silver.

Green grass edges the darkening lake
and red clouds stream from the east.

All day long, the orioles call,
and cranes brush tall white clouds.

Once dry, these wildflowers bend and, there
where the wind is sweeping, fall.

Poem for My Brother Returning to My Farm

Wandering has been my way,
and you alone stayed with me.

You knew the shortcuts by the streams,
the secret ways back home.

Count the ducks and geese at twilight
and latch the old wood gate.

When the bamboo grove is thin, plant more—
the season soon grows late.

Tu Fu (712–770)

Spring Homecoming

Through tall bamboo the mossy path
winds down to the easy river.

Flowers bloom beneath the eaves
of the ancient wide-thatched hall.

After months away,
I come back home in spring,

leaning on my cane
to look at flowers and stones,

bringing my wine jar down
to walk and drink on the beach.

Gulls swim and dive in the distance,
swallows wrestle with the wind.

The world's ways are difficult, indeed,
but every life has its limits.

Sobering up, I drink again:
stoned, I finally feel at home.

Lone Wild Goose

Alone, the wild goose refuses food and drink,
his calls searching for the flock.

Who feels compassion for that single shadow
vanishing in a thousand distant clouds?

You watch, even as it flies from sight,
its plaintive calls cutting through you.

The noisy crows ignore it:
the bickering, squabbling multitudes.

I Stand Alone

A falcon hovers at the edge of the sky.
Two gulls drift slowly up the river.

Vulnerable while they ride the wind,
they coast and glide with ease.

Dew is heavy on the grass below,
the spider's web is ready.

Heaven's ways include the human:
among a thousand sorrows, I stand alone.

The Thatched Hut

When Barbarians overran the city,
I abandoned my old thatched hut.

But now the city is peaceful once again,
and at last I can come back.

The rebellion broke in a flash—
planned to be ruthless and sudden.

With our general off to visit the court,
his hirelings conspired,

they sacrificed a beautiful white stallion
and swore their oath in its blood.

Some rode west to conscript an army;
some closed the road to the north;

some, especially vile,
even named themselves to office.

But when Barbarians challenged their power,
these traitors were afraid.

In the west, the army mutinied,
rebel killing rebel—

who could have guessed their deaths
would come from their own cruel legions—

all decent people grieved
at a world plunged into chaos.

Petty officials multiplied,
and thousands became their victims.

Their terrorist hirelings, indiscriminate,
murdered innocent and innocent alike,

amused themselves with torture
performed to chamber music

and ordered death with a laugh.
The streets were sewers of blood.

You still can hear their cries
there where the axes fell.

The rebels plundered freely,
stealing horses, enslaving women,

and where was the empire then?
We were afraid and brokenhearted.

I had no choice—I ran.
And longed three years for the coast.

Arrows filled the air above the Yangtze.
And I longed for the Five Lakes region.

A life away is not a life—
I return to attack my weeds.

Inside the gate, four strong pines.
I stroll through my bamboo grove.

My old dog yips and leaps,
darting in and out of my robe.

Tu Fu (712–770)

My neighbors rush out to greet me
with bottles of sweet rice wine.

Even the governor sends greetings
by an official to assess my needs.

Our whole village celebrates,
my neighbors and my friends,

but still there's no peace in the world.
We honor more soldiers than poets.

Between the wind and the dust,
is there room for a poor man's life?

I live like a parasite—
happily, happy just to be alive.

If I've not earned my food and wine,
let all the worst be mine.

After the Harvest

The rice is cut and clouds glisten in the fields.
Facing Stone Gate, the river is low.

Winds shriek, ripping leaves from shrubs and trees.
At dawn, the pigs and chickens scatter.

Out of the distance, I hear the first sounds of battle.
The woodcutter's song is over. Soon he will leave the
      village.

Homeless and old, I long for a word from the homeland.
A wanderer, I place my trust in the world.

Moon, Rain, Riverbank

Rain roared through, now
the autumn night is clear.
The water wears a patina of gold
and carries a bright jade star.
Heavenly River runs clear and pure,
as gently as before.

Sunset buries the mountains in shadow.
A mirror floats in the deep green void,
its light reflecting the cold, wet dusk,
dew glistening,
freezing on the flowers.

Running from Trouble

Barely fifty, but already my face is old, hair white.
I traveled this whole coast fleeing the state.

Rough cloth saved my shivering bones
as I roamed the awful cold.

Thus began the years of my disease.
Everywhere, people were mud and ash.

Between heaven and earth,
there's nowhere a body is safe.

I see my wife and children follow.
We sigh for mutual sorrows.

My old home gone to weeds,
and all my neighbors scattered,

we may never find the road back home.
We add our tears to the river.

A Broken Boat

All my life, I've dreamed of lakes and rivers.
I've had that little boat for years.

I used to row in the creek every day
out beyond my brushwood gate.

But then I fled the rebellion
and longed for my hut in the hills.

All my neighbors vanished.
The bamboo grove's grown tall.

With my boat a year in the water,
I don't dare tap its bottom.

Other travelers go west on easy wings.
Even the river moves easily, flowing east.

I could repair my poor old boat,
or I could easily buy another.

Why have I always run from trouble?
Even in my cottage, there's no peace.

Facing the Snow

New ghosts weep over lost battles.
Alone and cold, I recite a litany of woes.

Heavy clouds rumble into the sunset,
quick snow dancing in the winds.

Imperfect, the smith's new ladle lies discarded,
but his fire still throbs red.

No news. Are all the provinces still there?
I write out my sorrows in air.

Traveler's Pavilion

Sunrise brightens my autumn window.
Winds have once again stripped trees.

The morning sun slips between cold mountains.
The river runs through last night's mist.

Our court makes use of everything it can,
but what's the use of a sick old man?

And what of my one life remains,
rising or falling on autumn winds?

On a Portrait of a Falcon

Wind and frost on ordinary silk,
and this wonderful gray falcon.

Body tensed, he eyes a rabbit,
watching his own flanks as well.

On a ring the size of a finger,
he hangs, waiting for a call.

Oh, he will bring down the little birds,
leaving feathers and blood on the plains.

Homage to the Painter General Ts'ao

As Lady Wei's star pupil, your calligraphy
was compared to General Wang's.

Impervious to old age, while you painted,
prosperity slipped past you like clouds.

Sleepless Nights

The bamboo cold creeps into my room.
Moonlight over the wilds floods the yard.

The dew grows heavy, dripping,
and only here and there some stars.

Fireflies shine their own lights, flying the dark.
Perched birds call out across the water.

The world's affairs are snarled in war.
I regret the night is wasted.

Night in a Room by the River

Evening rises toward the mountain trails
as I climb up to my high chamber.

Thin clouds lodge along the cliffs.
A lonely moon rocks slowly on the waves.

A line of cranes flaps silently over,
and, far off, a howling pack of wolves.

Sleepless, memories of war betray me:
I am powerless against the world.

Night Thoughts While Traveling

Thin grass bends on the breezy shore,
and the tall mast seems lonely in my boat.

Stars ride low across the wide plain,
and the moon is tossed by the Yangtze.

What is fame and literary status—
the old and infirm should leave office.

Adrift, drifting: what is left for the lone gull
adrift between earth and heaven.

A Summit

Biting winds, dark clouds, monkeys howling in the trees.
Gulls circle slowly over sands.

Crumple of windblown fallen leaves.
The river laps at the shore.

Always, in autumn, away from home,
I endure this long, steep climb.

Sick and alone, failure turned my temples snowy.
I suffer and I grumble: giving up the wine.

To My Younger Brother

(of whom I've learned nothing in four years)

I've heard from strangers you may be living
in a Hangchou mountain temple.

The dusty winds of war prolong our separation.
I've spent another autumn beside the Yangtze and the
    Han.

My shadow passes under trees filled with screaming
    monkeys,
but my heart turns down toward the dragons at the river
    mouth.

When spring waters rise, may they carry me down
to search for you in the east where the white clouds end.

By Yangtze and Han

Wandering beside rivers, I remember my home
between heaven and earth, an aging exiled scholar.

Only a smeared ghost of a cloud
and a pale moon in the long night sky.

The sun has set in my heart.
Autumn winds rise up around my sickbed.

Even the old horse has its stall in the barn
though he's too old for the road.

At the Thatched Hall of the Ts'ui Family

It is autumn at the grass hut on Jade Peak.
The air is cool and clear.

Temple bells and chimes echo from the canyons.
Fishermen and woodsmen wind over sunset trails.

We fill our plates with chestnuts gathered in the valley
and rice grown in the village.

For what, Wang Wei?
Bamboo and pine, silent, locked behind a gate.

Facing the Snow

Northern snows invade the city,
northern clouds have frozen all the homes.

Hard winds mix leaves with snow,
cold rains erase the flowers.

Once again, no money, I wonder
if I could get wine on credit.

But without a friend to share it,
I'll wait for sunset and the crows.

Six Choruses

1.
The sun rises over eastern seas;
clouds rise over the muddy northlands.

Kingfishers sing from tall bamboo.
Egrets dance on the sand.

2.
Mist drifts down as flowers fall;
bees and butterflies rise.

What should I do if someone comes
to visit the shade where I roost?

3.
Dig a well and make a rope of hemp,
and bamboo pipes for drainage.

The boats are knotted at their moorings.
Crooked pathways bind the village.

4.
Rains fall at the river mouth;
low sun embraces the willows.

Dark birds meet near broken nests;
a white fish leaps from grass floating in the river.

5.
Bamboo overtakes this hut's poor walls
and cane blooms in the courtyard eaves.

The river takes the sun's soft strands
to weave with slender reeds.

6.
The moon floats across a river of sky,
but this river is illusion—a cloud of mist in flowers.

The silent roosting bird understands the Tao:
sails don't know where they go.

Heading South

Spring returns to Peach Blossom River
and my sail is a cloud through maple forests.

Exiled, I lived for years in secret, moving on
farther from home with tearstains on my sleeves.

Now old and sick, at last I'm headed south.
Remembering old friends, I look back north a final time.

A hundred years I sang my bitter song,
but not a soul remembers those old rhymes.

Poems of Po Chu-i, Yuan Chen, and Others

Li Yi (749–ca. 829)

Listening to a Flute at Night near the City Wall

The sands stretch away like snow
under the shadows of Mount Hui-lo.

The moon is cold as ice
now the enemy has surrendered.

From which direction,
that solitary flute?

A thousand soldiers listen,
and dream of home.

Meng Chiao (751–814)

Despair

Despise poetry, and you'll be named to office.
But to love poetry is like clinging to a mountain:

frozen, holding tight, facing death,
days of sorrow followed by sorrow.

The bourgeoisie are jealous of those
who love poetry: they flash teeth like knives.

All the old sages are long since dead,
but bureaucrats still gnaw their bones.

Now I'm frail, dying like a frond.
All my life I sought a noble calm,

a calm I could never achieve.
And the noisy rabble mocked me.

Elegy

We carved our names
in a courtyard near the river

when you were the youngest
of all our guests.

But you will never see
bright spring again,

or the beautiful apricot
blossoms that flutter past

the open temple door.

Liu Yu-hsi (772–842)

Blacktail Row

Grass grows wild by Red Bird Bridge.
At sunset, swallows rise over Blacktail Row,

bending wings over once-great homes,
dipping over the hovels of the poor.

After Reading Lao Tzu

"One who speaks does not know; one who knows does
     not speak."
Thus I have been instructed by the Old Master.

If you tell me the Old Master was one who knew, I ask,
Why did he write five thousand words to explain it?

To Yuan Chen

I came a thousand miles to share your dream
after two long years alone.

Remember where we strolled and talked—
below the steps, hidden in the bamboo grove?

On a Portrait of the Poet

I didn't know my own face
until it was painted by Li Fang.

Quietly, I study the bones, the spirit.
He must be a man from deep in the mountains.

The reed willow rots quickly.
The wild deer's heart is impossible to tame.
Why have I walked these red palace stairs
in servitude for five long years?

Uncompromising, inflexible character
makes it difficult to share the world.

Those who are called nobles
give me good reason to fear.

I must resign and seek retreat to save
what's left of this body of clouds and streams.

Night Duty in the Palace, Dreaming of a Hsien-yu Temple

Tired of my writing brush, I gazed out the window:
bamboo and pine were perfectly still.

At moonrise, a slight breeze came up,
like on those long-ago nights in the hills.

As though dreaming, I returned to the Hsien-yu Temple
near my home in the southern mountains.

When the palace water-clock awakened me,
I thought it was the laughter of mountain streams.

Po Chu-i (772–846)

To a Young Widow

Her window ringed by moonlight,
light frost on her screen,

her low bed pale and cold
in flickering candlelight:

late moonlight and early frost
on Swallow Tower.

Autumn brings long, long nights
to one who sleeps alone.

Reading Yuan Chen on a Boat

By candlelight, I read your poems.
It is almost dawn when I finish.

I rub my weary eyes
beside the guttering candle.

I sit motionless
in the predawn dark,

listening to wind-driven waves
lapping at the bow.

Cold Night

At midnight, in a cold bed, I cannot sleep.
Incense and fire burned out, my tears turn to ice.

My shadow my only companion,
I will not turn down the light.

River Flute

Downriver, someone plays
a bamboo flute at midnight.

Note by note, I'm transported
back into my youth at home.

Listening, I feel my thin hair
quickly turning white:

still growing old, still
sleepless, still alone.

Anonymous (T'ang dynasty)

In the Shadows of the Wu-t'ung Tree

The pale moon disappears
when cold autumn winds begin to blow.
Waiting, I wonder if he will . . .

waiting, pacing
the shadows of the wu-t'ung tree,
counting falling tears.

Liu Tsung-yuan (773–819)

Snowy River

The birds have vanished
      from a thousand mountains.
On a thousand trails,
      not a single human sign.

A little boat,
      a bamboo hat and cloak—
the old man, alone,
      fishing the snowy river.

White Dress

Light rain settles this white dust,
and her perfume penetrates thin walls.

Her jade-white body slips into a jade-white gown.
The embroidery is beautiful, but sad.

She blossoms like a pear against an ivory couch.
A silk blouse and green skirt

hang in the smoky incense of aloe.
Why do I waste time painting early morning clouds?

Oriole

Her dress is soft green and deep scarlet.
Her rouge is smeared, her hair undone.

She is a misty lotus kissed by dawn,
a rain-soaked flower weeping for the sun.

A flicker at her lips? A smile perhaps?
Her fragrance is not perfume.

Her eyes flare up at her mother
who introduces this young man.

Yuan Chen (779–831)

Peach Blossoms

Infinite peach-blossom shades,
her rouged and powdered cheeks.

Spring breezes help her break my heart,
blowing peach petals from her dress.

Letter Smuggled in a Fish

Your letter unfolds and unfolds forever.
I flatten it with my hands to read:

tearstains, tearstains and a trace of rouge
where it must have touched your cheek.

When We Are Apart

I've seen the sea—how could I settle for a river?
There are no other clouds after you've seen Mount Wu.

These elegant gardens don't move me now—
because of my discipline. Because of you.

Three Dreams in Chiang-ling

1.
When you were alive, we often dreamed together,
but you couldn't live in my dream world.

Now death has come between us
and I'm left to dream alone.

My dreams will get me nowhere,
but there's no other way to meet.

What does it mean
when you return in dreams?

You wear the old familiar clothes,
but your face has a pallor like clouds.

You say nothing of death.
But you always say good-bye.

Your sewing is strewn around you
and the bedding and drapes are folded.

You touch our daughter and weep
and pass her back to me,

our only child,
and you remind me she is young,

and weep for our lack of sons.
"Little joy in the trivial,"

Yuan Chen (779–831)

you say, "and you can barely care for the family
with your duties to your office.

How can you tend to business?
When duty divides others,

the servants abuse their young.
Take care. Stay home.

And when you go away,
be careful whom you trust."

Your words are clotted with sobs
that fill my eyes with tears.

Awakened by my grief,
I freeze

on my moonlit bed in the dark.
Insects click in the grass outside.

Heart and head divided, did I
dream I was only dreaming?

I search my mind for your face
until I weep from exhaustion.

Our life together is over.
I grieve in every dream.

Our little daughter loved you,
and now I must leave her, too.

Ch'ang-an is more distant than the sun—
beyond mountains, clouds, and rivers.

Even if I had wings,
this net of grief would snare me.

The tears I weep tonight
are also shed for the living.

Your spirit comes to Yellow Springs,
the river stirs old memories.

How can I love such pain,
how can I live in a dream?

Dawn slowly breaks.
The river moans under branches.

2.
Deep in a cave in the ancient cemetery
I buried my precious jade flower.

The mound door had been stolen
and grass grew in smoky tangles.

I sat on the mound all day.
I'd left all hope in the village.

I wake in a moonlit bed.
Winds and waves rock the water.

3.
Your bones have turned to dust.
My heart has burned to ashes.

What happened to our allegiance?
Three nights you've come into my dreams.

Water flows on forever.
Nothing can catch the clouds.

The morning sun arrives:
birds fly up in pairs.

Dreaming of My Wife

The candle burned out, my boat is windblown.
You ask about my southern sailing:

I sat awake all night in silence,
waves pounding on the lake.

Retirement

Life is lovely in seclusion
near tall pines in remote mountains.

I wander with clouds all day,
all night I follow the moon.

A world in a teapot:
fame is a silly dream.

Across the sea,
the thousand-year-old crane

lingers in the city,
but one day may return.

Remembering

I daydream, melancholy at the windowsill—
memories I will never tell—

our passion in the late-night hours,
our tearful good-byes at dawn.

Mountains and rivers divide us,
and I've given up hoping for rain.

Divided, I dream of you today—
I even embrace the pain.

Bamboo Mat

I cannot bear to put away
the bamboo sleeping mat—

that first night I brought you home,
I watched you roll it out.

Elegy

Oh, loveliest daughter of Hsieh,
you married a hapless scholar
and spent your life with a needle,
patching his old clothes.

Yuan Chen (779–831)

He thanked you by selling your gold pins
for wine. He picked herbs
and berries for your meals,
and locust leaves for the fire.

Now that they pay me handsomely,
there's no offering I can bring
but this sacrificial mourning.
We used to joke about dying.

Now you are suddenly gone.
I gave all your clothes away,
and packed up your needlework—
I couldn't bear to see them.

But I extend your kindness toward our maid,
and bring you gifts in lonely dreams.
Everyone learns this sorrow, but none
more than those who once suffered together.

Alone and lonely, I mourn us both.
Approaching sixty, I know better men
who lived without a son, better poets
with dead wives who couldn't hear them.

In the dark of your tomb,
there is nothing left to hope for—
we had no faith in meeting after death.
Yet when I open my sleepless eyes,

I see through those long nights
the grief that troubled your life.

Empty House

I leave my empty house at dawn
and ride to my empty office.

I fill the day with busywork.
At nightfall, back to my empty house.

Moonlight seeps through the cracks.
My wick has burned to ash.

My heart lies cold in Hsien-yang Road,
under the wheels of a hearse.

Anonymous (T'ang dynasty)

Elegy

Cheek by cheek on our pillow,
we promised to love until green mountains fell,

until iron floats on the river,
and the Yellow River itself runs dry—

to love until Orion rises in the night
and the North Star wanders south.

We promised undying love until
the sun at midnight burns the sky.

Wang Fan-chih (T'ang dynasty)

Requiem

Houses in country and city:
as far as you can see, he built them all.

Now his relatives all gather to mourn,
thinking of money in the funeral hall.

Reclusive

My thatched hut's plenty
to hold off wind and dust,
even if I haven't a blanket
to cover my sleeping mat.

Friends come to visit
in the cold, and we huddle,
a few twigs and scraps for the fire,
my old bones growing brittle.

Cool wine in clay bowls,
my old battered zither,
a few strips of jerky,
and my company is happy.

"Ohhh," they sigh, and "Ahhh!"
They laugh hysterically.
They laugh at me.
They laugh.

Li Ho (791–817)

Lament for a Courtesan

Deep within the shadows,
her hall is hung with flowers,

willows tangled
in a fragrant mist.

Her golden plectrum picks
a song of phoenixes and fairies,

her hair like clouds
spread out across her pillow.

Her camphor incense dwindles.
She awaits Chou Yu the Handsome,

hoping he will ride
the west wind's fiercest steed.

Song: Green Water, Singing Girl

This wind is easy, the moon pleasant,
but where is the singing girl, poor Hou?

Because her beauty breaks the hearts of men,
she grows sad and shamed.

Li Ho (791–817)

Does she gather lotuses by East Lake,
pick cattails by South Lake?

With no hope of gaining a sister-in-law,
she garners the tokens of her sorrow.

Drinking All Night, Sleeping All Day

Rosy from wine, she rises
as light rises in the east.

Her sash is half untied.
The stars are fading.

From the garden, crows caw,
"Drunken princess!"

Flowers bend under heavy dew.
She draws her morning water

with a windlass of jade
and a rope of hand-tied silk.

Her face is powdered,
but still flushed faintly purple.

Drinking all night, sleeping all day,
she hasn't a care in the world.

Behind silk curtains, she sleeps
like an emperor's daughter.

Li Ho (791–817)

Days of Rain

Who is he, this regretful man
come to suffer autumn in Ch'ang-an?

Young, I learned a traveler's sorrows—
I wept in my sleep till my hair turned white.

My bony horse gets moldy hay
as rain turns to slush in the gutters.

South Palace is dark behind blinds,
its sundials blank under water.

My mountain home lies east,
under a thousand miles of clouds.

Sleeping with a scabbard for a pillow,
I dream a life as a soldier.

The Lute Player

I saw Hsiao-lien by the river
and asked her to play her lute.

Although I paid her little,
she eased my melancholy.

Now her skirt hangs loose,
wet flowers in her hair.

Her jade bracelet is cold,
the lute strings heavy.

Her horse is saddled.
She rides for the palace at Ch'i.

Life at the Capital

With too much hope,
I galloped through the city gate.

Now in the lonely capital,
my heart accepts its fate:

alone, with no one
to confide in,

I sing only to
freezing late fall winds.

Melancholic

She lies tonight
        a thousand miles away,
her night-black hair spread out
        like all the heavens.

Who was that shadow
    lying there inside
her shadow until
    the candle vanished?

The bamboo sleeping mat
    I wove for her
is damp, pungent with the sweat
    of their passion.

A Country Road

Fragrant fireweed grows in the rain.
Tonight, August near the mountains,

they bloom in lonely places.
Moss and grasses slowly overtake

this stony rutted road
I carved eight years ago.

Tu Mu (803–852)

Departing in Early Morning

My quirt dangles freely.
I trust my horse.

Traveling mile after mile
without as much as a cock crow,

dozing off as I
pass through the woods,

I wake with a start
when leaves begin to fly.

Li Shang-yin (813–858)

Alone Beside the Autumn River

All spring, my sorrows grew like lotus leaves.
Now they wither as my autumn sadness grows.

Grief is as long and wide as life.
Watch the autumn river. Listen to it flow.

From the Heights

I drag my heavy heart
up to these dazzling heights:

this beautiful, beautiful sunset!
And then the onrushing night.

The Rise of Tzu Poetry

To the Tune: Southern Song

Her eyebrows are arched willows,
her cheeks the color of peaches.

Light silk clings to her lovely breast.

O beautiful!
—white lotus rising from the water.

To the Tune: The Water Clock

Incense burns to embers in the burner.
A red candle casts a glow across the walls.

It is autumn. My makeup
is a mess, my hair disheveled.

Pillow and bed are shivering cold.
Another long night lies ahead.

Wei Chuang (836–910)

To the Tune: Beautiful Barbarian

Our sad farewell at the red tower—
I just can't shake the memory.

The lamp was fragrant,
the curtain rolled halfway
that night I said good-bye.

The moon was dying.
You said goodbye through tears.

On a lute patterned with kingfisher feathers
someone played "The Oriole Song,"
and you begged me to return.

Your face was a perfect flower
framed by a window painted green.

Wei Chuang (836–910)

Against Conscription

In what dynasty, under what emperor,
did we live without war?

And in every war
every man dreamed of peace.

And now the farmer
finds more bones than soil.

And here comes the draft board,
wanting more bodies.

Li Hsun (855–930)

To the Tune: The Wine Spring

Eternal autumn rain—evening sounds
die out among the dying lotuses.

How can she bear to listen?
Wine has muddied her thinking.

And yet her thoughts fall like rain
after the candle has guttered,

after the incense has burned.
Almost at dawn,

when the misty rain is coldest,
it steals in through her screen.

To the Tune: The Wine Spring

Rain falls on fallen flowers
perfuming the edge of the pond

where she grieves through
a long separation.

When the song closes,
she closes her silver screen.

Night and day, sailboats
depart for the land of Ch'u.

In her pain, she tunes her lute.
The melody carries her grief,

and words vibrate in the strings,
words she cannot bear to sing.

Hsueh Chao-yun (900–932)

To the Tune: In the Hills

At Ch'ang-men, the grass is green,
jade stairs shimmering under dew.

Mist softens the moonlight.
East winds drown a sorrowful flute.

The water clock marks time.
Outside, orioles greet the dawn.

I wake in the night
grief-stricken, in tears,

exhausted, just exhausted.
My grip crushes my robe.

Once again, my mind settles over you
like dust settles over our scrolls.

Oriole Song

Ch'ing Ming—Clear Bright—
rain has left the sky clean and clear.
I made my name in this season.
Under my silk saddle
my pony dances through the mud
and my whip stays hidden in my sleeve.

Flowers always bloom together,
and men compete in their praise.
Each saddle bears its ornament,
each bridle a beaded design.
Reluctant to leave,
this sunset ends my pleasure:

I ride the old roads that enter
deep mist and tall grasses.

Hsu Hsuan (916–991)

Lu-lung Village, Autumn

Refusing worldly worries,
I stroll among village strollers.

Pine winds sing, the evening village
smells of grass, autumn in the air.

A lone bird roams down the sky.
Clouds roll across the river.

You want to know my name?
A hill. A tree. An empty drifting boat.

Li Yu (937–978)

To the Tune: Beautiful Lady Yu

Spring blossoms, autumn moon—
how long before they perish?

How much past can
one lone man endure?

Last night, the east wind
entered my tower again.

It breaks my heart, seeing my lost
country in this cold, clear moonlight.

Jade steps and intricate balconies
remain. But the faces have all changed.

Just how much grief
can one lone man endure?

As much as the east-flowing river
swollen with the waters of spring.

To an Ancient Tune

Once I gorged myself in a peach grove,
singing, dancing to the songs of phoenixes.

I remember our good-byes, so long ago,
mingling her tears with mine.

My hand touched her arm at the door—
like a dream, like a dream.

Now the moon's disappeared.
All the peach blossoms fall,

and heavy mist blankets the world.

Springtime South of the Yangtze

Misty waves in the distance
keep a thousand miles between us.

East winds spread the scent
of duckweed's sweet, white blossoms.

The sun slowly descends
beyond these floating islands.

And remembrance, that big spring river,
flows on and on, forever.

Liu Yung (987–1053)

Song

It's the wine, this ache, this longing.
It gets better and better until
I think I'm at Heaven's Gate!

I long to hold you once again,
your fragrance, your warmth I lean on
as you sleep in my arms till noon.

It's wine that makes me crazy!
Your embroidered duck-down quilt
tossing on its own red waves.

Song

She lowers her fragrant curtain,
wanting to speak of her love.

She hesitates, she frowns—
the night is over much too soon!

Her lover is first into the bed,
warming the duck-down quilt.

She lays aside her needle
and drops her rich silk skirt,

eager for his embrace.
But first he asks one thing:

that the lamp remain burning
so he can see her face.

Song

After the eating, the drinking, the singing,
we shared your red down quilt—

I still remember the bedroom where we met.
We should have stayed together.

How could we know our casual love
would grieve us so in our parting?

Song

Because spring brings miserable green and painful red,
my heart is moved by nothing.

When the sun ascends the flowers
and orioles stream through the willows,

I remain in bed, wrapped
snug in a perfumed blanket.

Liu Yung (987–1053)

My face is a mess.
My hair is a mess.

But I'm too shiftless to care.
What can I say?

That my cruel paramour
has left me? That he's sent no letter?

I should have known this would happen.
I wish I'd locked away his saddle.

I should have locked him in his study,
and brought him brush and paper,

and made him chant his poems.
We could have had days together,

rather than being divided.
I would put aside my sewing

to snuggle up against him.
And the best years of our lives

would not have gone for nothing.

Lament

Late autumn, a brief shower
has dampened the balcony garden.

Near the door, chrysanthemums wither.
Trees near the well are starving.

Sadly, I look out on the Yangtze River Gorge
where dark clouds obliterate the sun.

When Sung Yu suffered, he came here alone
to watch the autumn river

or wander in hills where distant roads all vanish.
He grieved until he couldn't bear the river any longer.

Suddenly, cicadas cry among dead leaves,
and crickets call and answer.

Days pass, slow as years inside this empty house.
Change comes slowly,

but the night at least brings silence,
and the transparent River of Heaven,

and the brightness of the moon.
Thought follows thought night after night.

It's the same old thing as the years
continue to wound me with memories of our past.

With neither name nor appointment,
I squandered years hanging around red towers.

The capital was fine when I was young—
eating all night, drinking all day,

wild friends and exotic women toasting,
lingering near the music.

Since then, time has clicked by like a shuttle.
The good old days are a dream.

Hidden in mist and water,
my journey continues forever.

Fame and money? Rags and empty dreams.
When I think back, I could weep.

Now a late chill settles in
on the dying notes of a horn.

I close my shutters and snuff the lamp.
An hour before dawn,

I hold my shadow in my arms
and do not sleep.

Cicada Song

The cicada's autumn song is lonely,
evening in the pavilion after a sudden storm.

At a banquet near the gate, I failed to pay attention.
I long to stay, but soon my boat will be ready.

Quietly choking back our tears,
we walk, hand in hand,

eyes searching one another's eyes.
I will cross a thousand misty waves before I stop.

Evening dark shuts down the southern sky.
People have always grieved at parting.

But how can I endure this long desolate autumn?
Where will I be tonight when I wake from drunken sleep?

A willow bank. Dawn's breeze.
Under a waning moon.

I will be gone for years,
and these beautiful days will be gone, and although

a thousand romantic dreams may overcome me,
with whom could I possibly share them?

Yen Shu (991–1055)

Song

An old song with new words,
a cup of clear wine—

last year's weather haunts
old towers and pavilions.

The sun sinks below the world.
Will it ever return again?

Nothing can be done
to delay the flowers' falling.

When the swallows come
like old friends returning,

I pace this fragrant
narrow garden path alone.

Mei Yao-ch'en (1002–1060)

The Lice

A poor man's clothes are ragged, quick to soil,
quick to soil and hard to get free of lice.

Between belt and skirt they nest,
climbing stealthily toward the collar.

So well hidden; how can I possibly find them?
They dine on my blood and nestle in my skin.

My life has give-and-take enough,
why poke my nose into yours?

Mei Yao-ch'en (1002–1060)

Necessities

All I want from this life
is poetry and wine.

I get depressed when I go
a single day without them.

Fame and status mean nothing.
My storage room is empty,

my stew pot freezing cold.
I don't give a damn.

Cold, hungry, my wife and kids
grow angrier by the day.

At war with the world,
I want only to write and to drink.

That is all I know
and all I need to know.

Ou-yang Hsiu (1007–1072)

A Cutting

I followed the winding path
past green moss and green courtyard willows

to meet her where we'd often met before.
But her bamboo curtain remained rolled closed.

So here am I, obvious in moonlight,
and nowhere to hide but in flowers.

Is our affair finally over?
Our last tryst was a disaster.

The water clock marks midnight.
I toss pebbles onto the balustrade:

no answer. But I hear from behind her curtain
the sound of busy scissors.

Wang An-shih (1021–1086)

Working for the Government

After spring snow, the capital's a city of mud.
I ride slowly toward sunset, going home.

You want an assessment of this life? Ha!
Thirty-nine long years, and not a thing to show.

Night Watch

Incense burned to ash in a bronze bowl.
The *drip, drip* of a distant water-clock.

The wind outside is a knife
slicing through the cold.

Suffering spring fever,
I lie awake, although dreaming.

The old, pale moon travels on.
Shadows of flowers climb the rail.

On Chung Mountain

A mountain stream in wild bamboo,
grass and flowers teased by mountain air.

We escape an all-day drizzle
huddled under thatched-roof eaves.

Not even a bird:
this mountain grows despair.

At Home

My cottage door opens on the water.
Beyond the little bridge,
a narrow road grows moss.

Willows shadow my house.
My neighbor's plum trees
perfume my tiny garden.

Spring Evening on Pan Mountain

Spring breezes erase the flowers,
leaving me in a state of pure *yin*.

This quiet downhill road leads by
a half-hidden bower where I'll make my bed.

Straw sandals, a walking stick—
I wander the world alone,

only a few northern birds pass by
like the memory of a beautiful song.

Hui-chu Temple, Mount K'un

Mountaintops emerge and then vanish
as lakes and rivers ebb and flood.

Trees and gardens almost float,
temples and gardens swarm across the hills.

A hundred miles of fishing boats,
a thousand hidden homes.

Visitors seldom come. Bittersweet,
sitting zazen with the monks.

Su Tung-p'o (1036–1101)

Climbing Yun-lung Mountain

Drunk, I scurry up a hillside
studded with sheep-sized boulders

until I stumble into a huge stone chair.
The sky is full of big white clouds.

Autumn winds carry work songs
up from trails far below

where workmen look up, astonished:
they clap their hands and yell.

At the Temple of Kuan Yin in the Rain

Silkworms enter cocoons: harvest time.
This rain soaks mountain and valley alike.

Berry picker and farmhand disappear:
no one in the fields at all.

The white-robed goddess, indifferent,
watches from her high hall.

Rain During the Cold Food Festival

This is my third Cold Food Festival
since I was exiled to Huang-chou.

Each parting spring, each year, I grieve.
Nevertheless, each passes—no regret.

This year there's pestilential rain,
the past two months dark as autumn.

I lie still, listening to cherry blossoms fall
into snow, pink and growing muddy.

Of what steals things in the dark,
the strangest arrives at midnight:

as though a young man went to bed
only to wake and find his hair turned white.

Remembering My Wife

Ten years ago, you died.
And my life ceased.

Even when I don't think of you,
I grieve. And with your grave

a thousand miles away,
there is no place for me

to give my grief a voice.
You wouldn't know me

if you saw me now,
me with snowy hair and a dusty face.

I dreamed myself home last night,
and saw you through a window

as you combed out your hair.
When you saw me, we were speechless

until we burst into silent tears.
Year after year, I remember

that moonlit night we spent alone
together in hills of stunted pine.

Ch'in Kuan (1047–1100)

Sleepless

The long night is deep, deep as water.
Hard winds pummel this outpost.

A mouse cries near the lamp,
shattering my dreams.

Frosty before-dawn chills
invade my lonely bed. No sleep.

No sleep again. Outside,
horses cry and people rise.

From a Dream

Rain brings flowers to this road each spring,
flowers to paint the hills with colors.

I hike along a secret stream
among a thousand yellow orioles.

Clouds take shapes of dragon and snake,
soaring, turning in the air.

I lie in wisteria shade, so drunk
I don't even know directions.

Song

Pleading eyebrows, intoxicating eyes!
When I first looked at you, I knew my heart was lost.

Do you remember that time in the west—
your billowing, cloudlike hair,

your best silk stockings, your lilac tongue?
You said to me, "When was I treated so well?"

But before the clouds and rain,
east winds blew everything away.

I'm grieving still,
but heaven doesn't hear.

Farewell Song

Faint clouds caress the mountains
where blue sky enters dry grass.

From the watchtower, a lone horn sounds.
Suddenly, I want to stop my little boat

and share a farewell cup of wine.
Our time together was a glimpse of paradise.

But that is futile to remember—
only the mist remains.

Ch'in Kuan (1047–1100)

A few cold crows grow smaller,
flying into the sun where the river

meanders through the village.
It breaks my heart, this long moment

when the perfume bag you gave me
is untied: our last love-knot severed.

Do you know me only by rumor,
a panderer among the courtesans?

Will you never see me again? For nothing,
we soak collar and sleeve with tears.

My heart breaks right there
where the city wall breaks my vision.

The night-lights flare.
Already the dark comes on.

Chou Pang-yen (1056–1121)

Peach Blossom Stream

There is no rest beside this stream, no love.
Once a lotus root is severed, it won't grow again.

Where once I waited by the red bridge rail
I walk through yellow leaves alone.

Mountains rise, green above the mist.
The red sun rides a wild goose into the dusk.

I drift like winds in a river of cloud.
Catkins after rain hold to the ground like love.

Chu Tun-ju (1081?–1159?)

To an Ancient Tune

Drunk on the blossoming plum,
once, long ago, I reveled all night.

Charming girls tugged my sleeves
for poems written on their scarves.

They quarreled over who might
fill my big jade cup with wine.

Nothing's the same, growing old—
no flowery girls, no wine.

All that's left to wet my gown
is an old man's tears alone.

I want to close my door and sleep
while plum blossoms blow like snow.

Li Ch'ing-chao (1084–1151)

To the Tune: Happiness Approaches

The wind has died.
Fallen petals drift in heaps.
Outside, the snow is almost red.
After the begonia blooms,
it is time to mourn the passing spring.

The wine is gone, our songs all sung,
our jade cups standing empty.
Once bright, the lamp is dying.
My dreams are sorry enough—
how can I bear the cuckoo's bitter cry?

To the Tune: Sands of the Washing Stream

I draw aside flowery bedside curtains
and lean my perfumed cheek
beside the gold mandarin incense burner,
turning my eyes discreetly—
he reads my very soul.

After he has passed,
I confess my passion in my journal:
I beg him boldly,
please come alone to me
when flowers cast moonlit shadows!

Li Ch'ing-chao (1084–1151)

To the Tune: Partridge Sky

Beautiful yellow cassia, so tender,
your heart seems far away, your perfume near.

You don't need a scarlet or a green.
Among all flowers, you are Queen.

The old plum grows envious,
chrysanthemums draw away—

among the autumn festivals,
they reign supreme.

The ancient poets never praised you.
They never really learned to see.

An End to Spring

At spring's end, I long for home,
feverish, my tangled hair uncombed.

All day, swallows squabble in the eaves.
Breezes bring the scent of roses through my screen.

To the Tune: Partridge Sky

Cold winter sunlight stuns the window.
The wu-t'ung trees despise the frost at night.

After all the wine, tea is bitter;
after the dream is gone,

incense is all that's left.
Autumn passes, and still the day is too long.

Others grieved across vast distances,
so I should endure the miles,

and, drunk, enjoy the brilliant yellow
chrysanthemums blooming along the wall.

To the Tune: Bodhisattva's Headdress

I thought it was spring—lazy sun, soft breeze,
a new light dress to ease my heart.

But this morning, rising, I was cold,
and the plum blossoms gathered for my hair were dead.

Is the old homeland changed?
Only the wine can ease my mind.

Sandalwood burned out, its incense gone,
only the sleep of wine remains.

To the Tune: Magnolia Blossoms

I bought a spray of blossoms from a vendor
who carried them on a pole.

Half open, glistening moisture
gathered like little teardrops

suggesting dew or morning rain
from clouds rising in the dawn.

So that he won't think these flowers
more lovely than my face,

I tie them in my long black hair
and ask him to compare.

To the Tune: Lips Painted Red

Secluded in my chamber:
a thousand threads of grief
are tangled in my stomach.

Once I loved the spring,
but spring has vanished
in torrents tearing away the flowers.

I lean from my balcony
as though searching for sorrow's end—
where *is* he—I look again:

dry grass meets the sky
and slowly overtakes
the long road he'll come home by.

To the Tune: Drunk in Flower Shadows

A long day of pining.
Light fog under heavy clouds,
camphor incense burned to nothing
in a gold dragon burner.

The ninth day of the ninth month passes.
By midnight, my curtained bed
and jade pillow are freezing.

I went through yellow dusk
to drink wine near the eastern wall.
A strange perfume filled my sleeves,
stunning me to the core.

Now the west wind lifts the curtains
and I grow frail
as a fading yellow flower.

To the Tune: Eternal Joy

Sunset pours its gold through jade-colored clouds.
But he has gone and heavy mist obliterates the willows.

Someone plays "Falling Plum Blossoms" on a flute,
and spring sadly passes.

The Lantern Festival signals calmer weather,
but tomorrow brings winds and rain.

My friend sends horse and carriage, but I can't bear
the company of old poetry-and-wine companions.

Long ago, in women's quarters, we celebrated
festivals all night in belts and necklaces of gold,

with emeralds in our hair—each outshining the other.
Now frail, windblown, and gray, I won't brave

an evening garden walk among those flowery girls—
I'll remain behind drawn curtains

eavesdropping, old—
listening to the heartbreak of their joy.

To the Tune: Happiness Approaches

The wind has died.
Fallen petals drift in heaps.

Outside, the snow is almost red.
After the begonias bloom,

it is time to mourn the passing spring.
The wine gone, our songs all sung,

our jade cups stand empty.
Once bright, the lamp is dying.

My dreams are sad enough.
How can I bear the cuckoo's bitter cry?

To the Tune: Plum Blossoms

The fragrance of red lotuses has faded.
Autumn settles at my door.

I loosen my robe and drift in an orchid boat.
Someone sent me love notes in the clouds,

in lines of returning geese,
in moonlight flooding the pavilion.

Flowers fade alone. Rivers flow alone.
Only our longing is shared.

Li Ch'ing-chao (1084–1151)

Sadness, grief, and worry
grow heavy in my eyes,

we are so long apart—
and settle in the bottom of my heart.

To the Tune: Spring at Wu Ling

The breeze has passed,
　　　　pollen dust settled,
and now the evening comes
　　　　as I comb out my hair.

There is the book, the inkstone, the table.
　　　　But he who was my life
is gone. It is difficult
　　　　to speak through tears.

I've heard it's always spring
　　　　at Wu Ling, and beautiful.
I'd take a little boat and drift
　　　　alone out on the water.

But I'm afraid a boat
　　　　so small would swamp
with the weight
　　　　of all my sorrows.

To the Tune: Butterflies Love Flowers

Warm rains and gentle winds
    have broken through the chill.
Willow eyes and peach buds
    press toward the sun.

I long for someone here
    to share poetry and wine.
But tears streak my rouge and silver
    phoenix pins are heavy in my hair.

In a gold embroidered gown,
    I hurl myself onto a mountain
made of downy pillows,
    and crush my favorite pin.

I hold myself in tired arms
    until even my dreams
turn black—
    first dark, then black.

Deep in the deepening night,
I trim the lamp's black wick.

Li Ch'ing-chao (1084–1151)

To the Tune: Sands of the Washing Stream

Beyond barred windows,
shadows cover the garden,

shadows slide over the curtain
as I play my lute in silence.

Distant mountains stretch the sunset,
breezes bring clouds and rain.

The pear blossoms fade and die,
and I can't keep them from falling.

To the Tune: Boat of Stars

Spring after spring, I sat before my mirror.
Now I tire of braiding plum buds in my hair.

I've gone another year without you,
shuddering with each letter—

since you've been gone,
even wine has lost its flavor.

I wept until it was autumn,
my thoughts going south beside you.

Even the gates of heaven
are nearer to me now than you.

To an Ancient Tune

You are like dust along the road.
I am like grass on the riverbank.

We meet, and our greetings are transparent:
even our footprints vanish.

As if burned by spring winds,
your face is flushed with wine.

Tears like autumn rains
until I cannot see.

After you bid good-bye,
will you still long for me?

Anonymous (Sung dynasty)

To the Tune: Beautiful Barbarian

The peonies are heavy with dew.
She pauses in the court to pick a flower,

then coyly asks her lover,
"Which do you think most pretty?"

Because he likes to tease,
he says, "I think perhaps the flower."

She pretends offense in any case,
crushes it, and throws it in his face.

Later Poems

Mural, Ch'ien-ming Temple

In this quiet alley, Ch'ien-ming Temple
has survived since the T'ang.

Now its famous mural is neglected—
half saved, half faded.

Bamboo leaves, stirred, sound like rain.
The old roof casts cold shadows.

As I approached, drumbeats called me.
I saddled my horse as sunlight flooded the balcony.

What comes and what passes?
The whims of fate.

Another priceless painting
flakes from a crumbling wall.

Anonymous (Yuan dynasty)

Song

Yellow dust drifts down the road to Ch'ang-an.
Broken gravestones litter the grounds at Mang-shan.

West winds toss a boat like a leaf
at Wu River Crossing.

The sun sinks into darkening trees.
History makes old men of us all—

it makes us old—melancholy ends
for these stout-hearted men.

Hu Chih-yu (1227–1293)

Love Song

Lazy flowers brew honey for the bees.
Light rains make mud for swallows.

In spring, under a green window,
I rise late.

What singing breaks
from an oriole at my gate!

Ma Chih-yuan (1260–1324)

Love Song

Clouds circle the moon,
breezes ringing wind chimes,
deepening my doubt.

I lit the lamp to write
my broken heart for you.
My sobbing blew it out.

In Autumn

Withered vines cling to the old tree
where crows call in the dusk.

Beyond the bridge and stream,
a few thin shanties.

A lean horse braves the road and west wind
as the sun slowly descends.

The broken man
wanders earth's farthest ends.

Evening Bells near a Temple

Under the thin smoke of winter,
the old temple remains quiet.

After a beautiful sunset,
the visitors have all gone.

On the west wind, three,
four chimes of the evening bell.

How can the old monk
concentrate on zazen?

Chang K'o-chiu (1265–1345)

At Waterfall Temple

These peaks gather like snowy swords,
the waterfall a curtain of ice on the cliff.

Gibbons in treetops toy with clouds.
Among blood red azaleas,

the cuckoo sings till it bleeds.
From within deep caves, wind gods scream.

Compared to the hearts of men,
these mountain wilds are tame.

Year's End

Her small feet walk a mossy path,
the moon a jade hook high above bamboo,

silent above the silent pavilion.
Time changes everything but sorrow.

A flash of fish in a dark pool,
birdsong welcoming the spring—

fallen plum blossoms
perfume the evening air.

Chang Yang-hao (1269–1329)

T'ung Pass

Masses of mountain peaks
and river waves as if in a rage—

the road through T'ung Pass
winds among mountains and rivers.

Looking west toward the capital,
I feel my heart begin to sink.

Where the thousand armies
of Ch'in and Han once passed,

I grieve: ten thousand palaces
ground into dust for nothing.

Dynasties rise, people suffer.
Dynasties fall, and people die.

Teng Yu-pin (ca. 1294)

Taoist Song

Empty bag of skin filling with desire,
skull packed full of blame!
I plotted for sons and daughters,
I slaved for our family name.

Do you understand?
I thought I could join the immortals!

Taoist Song

In white clouds, in green mountains,
in a thatched hut between summer and winter,
I pass time in simple conversation.
Tired, I doze among growing vines.

Do you understand?
Struggle follows struggle time after time.

Teng Yu-pin (ca. 1294)

Taoist Song

Heaven and hell are men's unhappy inventions,
as the ancients intended.

Good and evil get their due,
whether in this life or another.

Do you understand?
Don't primp like all the others
on the way to new incarnations!

Ch'iao Chi (dates unknown)

Love Song

Orioles and orioles,
      swallows and swallows—
everywhere, it is spring.

Flowers and willows,
      willows and flowers,
all grace, all charm.

And you are beautiful,
      so beautiful,
young, so young—

my perfect, graceful one.

Chao Shan-ch'ing (ca. 1320)

Autumn on the Riverbank

The corn grows large, the rushes tall,
as the shrubbery fades to yellow.

A pale green patina covers the sandbar.
Leaves fallen, even the mountains are pale.

Sandpipers hang in the wind above the river grasses,
ten thousand miles cloaked in autumn.

Soon, the sun will depart.
With a single cry, the wild goose passes.

Houses grow tall in the dark.

Hsu Tsai-ssu (ca. 1300)

On Love

I've been loveless all my life,
but now that love is mine

it drives me mad.
A body light as clouds,

a trembling willow of a heart—
my soul itself is gossamer thin.

Perfume loses all its magic
waiting for a wandering friend.

Heartache comes in its time:
whenever the lamp is low,

whenever the moon faintly shines.

Kuan Yun-shih (1286–1324)

Love Song

Fondling and snuggling,
we nestle in a mist-filled window.

Cuddling and cooing,
we sing on a moonlit pillow.

Listening, counting moments—
soon the watch will change.

As the fourth watch closes,
our passion rises.

But night flies,
and our frustration rises—

what could it hurt to steal
one more watch together?

Sung Fang-hu (ca. 1317)

A Traveler's Life

The rains are driven by stiff winds.
A small lamp burns on in the gloom.

I stir a few old embers in the stove,
my thin blanket frozen like winter iron.

My pillow is like ice.
This lonely, how can I keep away the cold?

Wang Po-ch'eng (ca. 1279)

Song of Parting

After you have gone,
your fragrance clings to the pillow.

After the dream has ended,
cold penetrates the covers.

My darkness grows heavy,
heavy as a mountain;

it grows deep,
deep as all the oceans.

Alone in a lonely bed, my thoughts
fall like rain, one upon the other.

Wang Yang-ming (1472–1529)

Magic City Monastery

High in the mountains,
Magic City Monastery teeters on the void.

Its towers reach almost to the gods.
The moon shines through cloudless autumn skies

as light rain darkens the world below.
A dragon glides down. Clouds will form its throne.

When the tiger returns to its cliffs,
winds will swarm in the forest.

Bless the kind old monk going about his way:
during evening rites, his chant is the only light.

Taoist Song

The old recluse lives under the cliff
in a shack among bamboo and pine.

At dawn, birds serenade him.
Evenings, the tiger's roar is a friend.

Notes on the Poets

Li Yen-nien (ca. 100 BCE) was a musician and songwriter in the court of Emperor Wu.

Cho Wen-chun was probably a "singing girl" who lived during the second century.

Ts'ao Ts'ao (155–200) was a powerful military leader, an outspoken anti-Confucian literary scholar who set many of his poems to music. His youngest son, Ts'ao Chih (192–232) also became an important poet.

Lu Chi (261–303) is most famous for his *Wen Fu, The Art of Writing,* a poem in essay form that has been studied by Asian poets for seventeen centuries. A revised edition of my 1987 translation is published by Milkweed Editions concurrently with *Crossing the Yellow River.*

Tzu Yeh may have been a single "wine-shop girl" or the poems known generally as "Tzu Yeh songs" may have multiple authors. They date from the 4th century CE. Because of the innovative style of composition—the *chueh-chu* or back-to-back couplets—they were probably written by a single author. The wineshop girl was rigorously trained in music, dance, calligraphy, history, and the arts of prosody and storytelling. Li Po claimed to have memorized all of her songs.

T'ao Ch'ien (365–427), also called T'ao Yuan-ming, was born in Kiangsi province and lived most of his life as an impoverished farmer. Rejecting the highly mannered style of his contemporaries, his poems reflect a serious mind infused with fundamental Confucian conviction combined with Taoist spirituality. Although his poems were neglected in his own lifetime, he became one of classical China's most venerated poets, often called "the grandfather of poetry."

Hsieh Ling-yun (385–433) was born to one of the most prominent families in southern China. He became the duke of K'ang-lo, and one of the most influential poets in Chinese history, bringing Buddhist practice and insight to classical "nature poetry," a term he would doubtless dislike. Nevertheless, he is, along with T'ao Ch'ien, one of the true "grandfathers" of Chinese poetry.

Hsieh T'iao (464–499) exercised substantial influence on the T'ang poets despite dying young and leaving only a small body of work. Is Li Po's famous poem of the same title a theft, homage, or merely another "take" on an already renowned poem? He was a provincial governor and an avid mountain climber who advocated wilderness journeys as a means to enlightenment.

Hsiao Kang (503–551) came from the royal family of the Liang dynasty, most of whom were deeply engaged in literary affairs.

Yu Hsin (513–581) was a poet whose melancholy poems on the destruction of the ancient city of Chin-ling inspired many T'ang poets, especially Tu Fu.

Wang Fan-chih (590–660) was immensely popular during the T'ang dynasty, but has since been largely forgotten. He was apparently abandoned in infancy in his birthplace in Honan. The influence of his plain-spoken style can be seen in the poetry of Han Shan and other poets.

Wang Po (ca. 650–676) was greatly admired for his technical dexterity.

Wang Chih-huan (688–742) was a master of the use of parallelism and a popular poet during the High T'ang period. The Heron Tower he describes is in Shansi province, a long way up the Yellow River from the sea.

Meng Hao-jan (689–740) was born in Hupeh province and spent his first forty years living on remote Lu-men Shan (Deer Gate Mountain). Failing his (*chin-shih*) examinations for office, he returned to seclusion in the mountains. His poems are often compared with those of his friends Wang Wei and Wang Ch'ang-ling, partly because all three poets sought the contemplative qualities of nature and composed in simple, direct syntax. He was greatly admired by both Li Po and Tu Fu.

Wang Ch'ang-ling (?–756) was, during his lifetime, considered the "supreme poet of the empire" and enjoyed far greater popularity than Li Po or other contemporaries.

Li Po (701–762) is China's most famous poet, one whose biography is thoroughly infused with the stuff of legend, much of which may have been generated by the poet himself. Imprisoned as a traitor, pardoned, exiled, celebrated, granted amnesty, he lived on the edge. He was a consummate panhandler and an epic drinker. Despite a complex vocabulary and rich, varied meters, he claimed to have never revised a poem. Legend says he drowned in the Yellow River, drunk, trying to embrace the reflection of the moon in 762.

Wang Wei (701–761) was perhaps China's first truly great Buddhist poet. Unlike the Taoist Li Po and the Confucian Tu Fu, he excelled as a courtier after having been imprisoned at the Bodhi Temple in the capital city of Ch'ang-an during the An Lu-shan Rebellion. He was admired as a poet, landscape painter and musician, and died while serving in the State Department in 761.

Tu Fu (712–770), the "Poetry Sage" (*shih sheng*) was born in 712 to a family that had once been part of nobility, but whose fortunes had declined. After failing his (*chin-shih*) examinations several times, he spent years wandering, living in poverty, a model of Confucian conduct and a poet whose inspiration came in large part from the suffering he observed during his travels, much of it the product of ruthless inscription and unfair taxation. His poetry went largely unacknowledged but by his friend Li Po and few others during his lifetime. Only 1554 of his ten thousand poems survive.

Li Yi (749–ca. 829) served in various military posts and in the courts of Emperor Hsien-tsung where he earned a reputation for being difficult. He was among the leading poets of his age.

Meng Chiao (751–814) was highly praised by Han Yu and other contemporaries. Unable or unwilling to conform to court society, his life was filled with poverty, failure, and bitterness. He turned to a classically Confucian stance embracing the virtues of suffering as a "scholar out of office."

Chang Chi (768–830), like Meng Chiao, spent a lifetime in poverty, but with the literary patronage of Han Yu and others, wrote many poems in the "folk-song style," denouncing social injustice, poems that would later influence Po Cho-i.

Liu Yu-hsi (772–842) was a leading poet of the mid-T'ang, often ranked with Po Chu-i and Yuan Chen. Banished to the provinces for satiric poems composed at the Hsuan-tu Monastery, he eventually rose to become a high court official.

Liu Tsung-yuan (773–819) was born and lived in the capital city of Ch'ang-an, but for fifteen years in exile in the south. His poems show the influence of early Ch'an (Zen) Buddhism.

Po Chu-i (772–846) is, along with Wang Wei, Li Po, and Tu Fu, among the best known of all Chinese poets in the West. He was unafraid of criticizing social injustice and was revered for his loyalty to friends. Like many of his contemporaries, he spent years in exile, but eventually achieved high position in the court and adopted the name "Lay Buddhist of Fragrant Mountain." He set the classical Chinese standard by writing ten thousand poems.

Yuan Chen (779–831) shared with his friend Po Chu-i a profound social conscience, and he also suffered banishment and exile for speaking out. A controversial poet (Su Tung-p'o called his poems "frivolous"), his elegies are among the most profoundly moving personal poems of the T'ang dynasty. A prose piece assumed to be autobiographical provided the story line which Yuan dynasty dramatists developed into *The Dream of the Red Chamber*.

Li Ho (791–817) was kept from achieving high office, and struggled with poor health. Although labeled a "mystical" poet because of his allusions to shamanistic practices and mythological themes, he was nonetheless poignant in social and political observations running throughout his poetry.

Tu Mu (803–852) claimed to have earned a reputation for hanging around courtesan's quarters, but was in fact a popular poet and governor of four districts. He lived happily in Hangchow at the mouth of the Yangtze River, where he was called "Little Tu" to distinguish him from Tu Fu.

Li Shang-yin (813–858) was orphaned while still very young, but was something of a prodigy. He wrote in many styles and on many subjects, often being charged with "obscurity," especially when he hid political allegory within poems on secret love.

Wen T'ing-yun (812–870), despite repeatedly failing his civil examinations (*chin-shih*), is generally considered the first great poet of the *tz'u* form.

Wei Chuang (836–910) was born in the capital district of Ch'ang-an, but was forced to flee to Lo-yang during a rebellion. He spent ten years as a wanderer before returning in 893, and becoming one of the country's most powerful political figures following the collapse of the T'ang dynasty.

Li Hsun's (855–930) ancestry leads back to Persians, but he nevertheless achieved great influence at the court of the independent state of Shu in tenth-century Szechuan. His younger brother was a well-known drug dealer, and Li Hsun authored a pharmacopoeia.

Hsueh Chao-yun (900–932) is known through only a handful of anthologized poems.

Li Yu (937–978) was the last ruler of the Southern T'ang dynasty and was revered for his painting and calligraphy as well as for his poetry. He is the first master of the *tz'u* style—new lyrics written to old tunes. Ill-suited to ruling the state, he managed to avoid war and encouraged Buddhism. He lost his wife and young son and was later captured, taken hostage by the Sung court, and given poisoned wine.

K'ou Chun (961–1023) is absent from the standard literary biographies. His poem is from a scroll.

Hsu Hsuan (916–991) was an accomplished editor who rose to the position of Supervising Censor before being banished to Shensi province.

Liu Yung (987–1053) was an accomplished musician and lyricist who worked as a junior secretary in a local administration in Chekiang, living in abject, resolute poverty. Most of his poetry was of the *man-tz'u* or "slow tune" genre, and his poems were sung throughout regional villages.

Yen Shu (991–1055) was born in Kiangsi, and achieved the highest rank in court, a rarity for southerners. Noted for his elegant literary style, his home became a gathering place for the literati.

Mei Yao-ch'en (1002–1060) endured terrible poverty, the premature death of his first wife and infant son, exile, floods, and repetitive invasions by barbarian armies. He annotated the Confucian classic *Art of War,* but found no success as a government official. Ou-yang Hsu admired his poetry greatly and became a close friend.

Ou-yang Hsiu (1007–1072) lost his father at four, grew up in extreme poverty, but became the quintessential statesman-scholar-poet thanks to the rise of printing and newly-available editions of Confucian classics. He was ingenious, inventive, gracious, and a patron to many budding poets, most notably Su Tung-p'o. He is, with Liu Yung, one of China's greatest love poets.

Chu Tun-ju (1081?–1159?) refused many court appointments before accepting a position as Judicial Intendant, and his poems often express his disillusionment with officialdom and nostalgia for carefree times.

Wang An-shih (1021–1086) served in a number of provincial posts before Emperor Shen-Tsung gave him genuine power, when Wang brought sweeping reforms in economic and social matters. He is often credited with being the first in the Sung dynasty to acclaim Tu Fu as the greatest of Chinese poets. He is counted among the "Eight Prose Masters" of the T'ang and Sung.

Su Tung-p'o (1037–1101), also known as Su Shih, was deeply schooled in the Taoism of Chuang Tzu and Lao Tzu before becoming devoted to the study of Ch'an Buddhism. As a political opponent of Wang An-shih, he suffered a number of defeats and banishments, but was renowned as a compassionate and benevolent administrator in the provinces. He is among the very greatest poets of the Sung dynasty.

Ch'in Kuan (1049–1100) was a follower of Su Tung-p'o and suffered banishment and exile. Fewer than a hundred poems survive, all poems of remorse or sorrow.

Chou Pang-yen (1056–1121) was a celebrated musician and songwriter and Director of the Imperial Music Bureau.

Li Ch'ing-chao (1084–1151) is one of China's greatest poets, a genius of the *tz'u*, one of the most influential critics of her age, and with her husband, compiler of an immense catalogue of stone and bronze vessels. The death of her husband at an early age was emotionally and socially devastating to a "liberated" Li Ch'ing-chao, perhaps China's first literary feminist. When her second husband proved abusive, she had the remarkable courage to leave him.

Yao K'uan was a Sung dynasty lyricist.

Li Yu (1125–1210) was born to a patriotic scholar-official in Chekiang, and raised to write poetry. His official career was constantly frustrated, but despite moving to and from many minor posts in various provinces, his literary labors spanned seven very productive decades. He wrote more than ten thousand poems.

Hu Chih-yu (1227–1293) lived during the end of the Southern Sung dynasty and the beginning of the Yuan dynasty.

Ma Chih-yuan (1260?–1334?) spent his youth in what is present-day Beijing. A popular playwright and poet, biographical information is questionable. He wrote seventeen plays, most noted for their melancholy themes.

Chang K'o-chiu (1265–1345) never rose above the lowest rank, but learned to love travel and making friends. He was devoted to principles of Ch'an Buddhism and Taoism, and his poems, noted for their elegance, were immensely popular.

Chang Yang-hao (1269–1329) served in many significant offices before retiring to write poems of nature and of the meaninglessness of official life. His name is associated with deep moral conviction and a sweeping sense of history.

Teng Yu-pin wrote during the early Yuan dynasty, circa 1280–1320. His "Taoist songs" could just as easily be called Zen songs.

Ch'iao Chi, Hsu Tsai-ssu, Chao Shan-ch'ing, Kuan Yun-shih (1286–1324), **Sung Fang-hu,** and **Wang Po-ch'eng** were early Yuan dynasty lyricists. No biographical information is available.

Wang Yang-ming (1472–1529) was the last great Confucian philosopher. He led the Ming revolt against the codified version of Chu Hsi's Neo-Confucianism. He was a compassionate official, a brilliant teacher, and his ideas are presented in Arthur Waley's *Monkey*.

Acknowledgments

Special Thanks to Paul Hansen, Irving Yu-cheng Lo, and J. P. Seaton for valuable instruction while reading various portions of this work. They are not responsible for my poetic license.

Thanks to: Harry and Sandra Reese at Turkey Press for publishing *Night Traveling* in 1985; Allan Kornblum at Coffee House Press for publishing *The Lotus Lovers* in 1985; Dennis Maloney at White Pine Press for publishing *Banished Immortal: Visions of Li T'ai-po* in 1987 and *Facing the Snow: Visions of Tu Fu* in 1988; Weatherhill for publishing *Endless River: Tu Fu and Li Po: A Friendship in Poetry* in 1993; Peter Turner at Shambhala Publications for publishing *Midnight Flute* in 1994.

Many of these poems were originally published by the following journals: *The American Poetry Review, Poetry East, Five Points, Willow Springs, Malahat Review, Jeopardy, Alaska Quarterly Review, Pequod, Crab Creek Review, Cream City Review, Northwest Review, Loblolly, Floating Island, Stone Lion Review, Wind Horse, Cafe Solo, Luna.*

About the Translator

Sam Hamill's celebrated translations include *The Art of Writing: Lu Chi's Wen Fu*; *The Essential Chuang Tzu* (with J.P. Seaton); *Narrow Road to the Interior & Other Writings of Bashō*; *The Spring of My Life & Selected Haiku by Kobayashi Issa*; *River of Stars: Selected Poems of Yosano Akiko* (with Keiko Matsui Gibson); *Only Companion: Japanese Poems of Love & Longing*; *The Erotic Spirit*; and *The Infinite Moment: Poems from Ancient Greek*. He is the author of a dozen volumes of original poetry, including *Destination Zero: Poems 1970-1995* and *Gratitude* (BOA, 1998), as well as three collections of essays, the most recent of which is *A Poet's Work*. He is Founding Editor of Copper Canyon Press, director of the Port Townsend Writers' Conference, and contributing editor at *The American Poetry Review*.

BOA EDITIONS, LTD.
NEW AMERICAN TRANSLATIONS SERIES

Vol. 1   *Illuminations*
Poems by Arthur Rimbaud
Translated by Bertrand
Mathieu with Foreword by
Henry Miller

Vol. 2   *Exaltation of Light*
Poems by Homero Aridjis
Translated by Eliot Weinberger

Vol. 3   *The Whale and Other*
Uncollected Translations
Richard Wilbur

Vol. 4   *Beings and Things on Their Own*
Poems by Katerina
Anghelaki-Rooke
Translated by the Author in
Collaboration with Jackie
Willcox

Vol. 5   *Anne Hébert: Selected Poems*
Translated by A. Poulin, Jr.

Vol. 6   *Yannis Ritsos: Selected Poems*
1938–1988
Edited and Translated by
Kimon Friar and Kostas
Myrsiades

Vol. 7   *The Flowers of Evil and Paris*
Spleen
Poems by Charles Baudelaire
Translated by William H.
Crosby

Vol. 8   *A Season in Hell and*
Illuminations
Poems by Arthur Rimbaud
Translated by Bertrand
Mathieu

Vol. 9   *Day Has No Equal but Night*
Poems by Anne Hébert
Translated by A. Poulin, Jr.

Vol. 10   *Songs of the Kisaeng:*
Courtesan Poetry of the Last
Korean Dynasty
Translated by Constantine
Contogenis and Wolhee
Choe

Vol. 11   *Selected Translations*
W. D. Snodgrass

Vol. 12   *Sea-Level Zero*
Poems by Daniela Crăsnaru
Translated by Adam J.
Sorkin with the poet and
others

Vol. 13   *Crossing the Yellow River:*
Three Hundred Poems from the
Chinese
Translated by Sam Hamill
with a Preface by W. S.
Merwin

Colophon

The publication of this book was made possible,
in part, by the special support of the following individuals:

Joseph Bednarik & Liesl Slabaugh,
Ronald & Susan Dow, Dane & Judy Gordon,
Robert & Willy Hursh, Richard Garth & Mimi Hwang,
George Keithley, William B. Patrick,
Stuart Rosenberg, Andrea & Paul Rubery,
Thomas R. Ward, Michael Wiegers,
and Pat & Michael Wilder.

This book was set in Monotype Dante fonts
by Richard Foerster, York Beach, Maine.
The cover was designed by Geri McCormick,
Rochester, New York.
Manufacturing was by McNaughton & Gunn,
Saline, Michigan.